UNPLANNING OUR PARENTHOOD

UNPLANNING OUR PARENTHOOD

Living Our Pro-Life Convictions with Freedom and Joy

Beverly Jacobson

Let the redeemed of the Lord tell their story—
Psalm 107:2

Let this be written for a future generation,
that a people not yet created may praise the Lord.
Psalm 102:18

For my husband, Ted, who has feared the Lord
and walked in obedience to Him…
on both mountaintop and valley pathways.
God honors your commitment to Him and to our family.
The blessings of Psalms 127 – 128 are indeed yours.
I love you more than words can say.

Inquiries should be directed to AnEssentialHarvest@gmail.com.

ISBN: 9781070113630
Imprint: Independently published

Contents

When I was in high school and college, I thought being pro-life revolved around politics and protests. In reality, it has much more to do with our everyday priorities than stepping into a voting booth or holding up signs. I've learned that different people may feel passionately about different aspects of pro-life issues—but the common thread is believing all humans have dignity because we are created in God's image.

Ultimately, it's about being pro-human.

As I write this story of our family's journey, the battle for the unborn rages more furiously than I've ever seen. That we as a nation could seriously engage in such heated debate over the killing of babies grieves and angers me. Science confirms what the Bible has told us all along[1]: those in the womb are human beings, knit together with a purpose for God's glory.

But let's be honest: there are times when being pro-life, being pro-human, is harder than we might think. Outwardly, my family and I have supported and affirmed the dignity of life in a variety of ways—for example:

- supporting adoptive and foster families;
- sponsoring vulnerable children;
- partnering with anti-trafficking ministries;
- visiting and honoring elderly citizens;
- donating to crisis pregnancy centers.

But inwardly my personal journey has been one of struggling to authentically live out these pro-life

---

[1] Psalm 139:13-18; Jeremiah 1:5; Ephesians 1:4, for example.

convictions. If I really, truly believe children are precious; if I truly believe God is the author of life and has purpose for every one of us; then what are the implications for me as a woman? As a wife? As a mother?

We never intended to have a large family. After nearly 22 years of marriage, our lives look far, far different from anything we imagined during those dreamy conversations leading up to the day we said "I do." (In fact, I'm pretty sure those discussions involved having two, maybe three children—and God has given us nine!) We have quite the collection of memories and experiences now. Some are breathtakingly beautiful. And some are born of such brokenness that my heart hurts just in the remembering. But remembering is good for the human soul. From Passover to the Lord's Supper, God commands His people to remember. And so, on these pages, I have remembered, praying the Lord who has been so gracious and patient with me will receive honor and glory.

I thought my heart was full when I gave birth to our firstborn. I couldn't imagine how I could possibly love another baby as much as I loved our sweet daughter. Then God gave us our first son. And I had the inkling of an understanding someone told me along the way: love doesn't divide when you add another child to your family—it multiplies. As God sent us each precious, unique child, I felt my love abound more and more, not only for my children, but also for the amazing husband I fell in love with all those years ago and for God my Father, whose heart surely understands what it's like to love all these children. He has billions and billions to love, after all!

Our journey as a family is OURS, and the story I have recounted here is descriptive—not prescriptive. My calling to live out my deeply held convictions comes from the Lord and is spoken to my heart, which is joined in marriage to my husband's. The two of us have made our family decisions prayerfully and through the guidance of the Holy Spirit. I pray our story will encourage and bless others—it is never my intention to tell others what they should or should not doing in the area of family planning. However, I stand firm when it comes to matters God Himself has clearly addressed. And since He alone is the author of Life, He alone has the right to give and take it.

"This day...I have set before you life and death, blessings and curses. Now choose life, so that you and your children may live and that you may love the Lord your God, listen to His voice, and hold fast to Him."
Deuteronomy 30:19-20a

Chapter 1
From Mosh Pit to Marriage

I met my husband in a mosh pit in the summer of 1995.

Really, it wasn't as wild as it sounds. Cornerstone Music Festival was a multi-day Christian event set up in the farmland of Bushnell, Illinois, featuring bands like Starflyer 59, Steve Taylor, The Crucified, and more. And our meeting wasn't entirely random. A mutual friend introduced us. I thought Ted was pretty cute and a rather good listener. And apparently, the way he tells it, Ted knew the weekend we met that he was going to marry me, despite the fact we lived hundreds of miles apart.

Six months later he flew to Wisconsin to hang out a few days and meet my family. It took him three days to muster up the courage to have the DTR (define the relationship) talk, but after staying up all night New

Year's Eve talking, we came to the conclusion that a long-distance relationship just might be worth attempting. We held hands and prayed God would direct our path, the first time I had ever begun a dating relationship in this manner. (I should have known at that point he was the one for me!)

My dad wholeheartedly approved, despite his initial impression when he first met Ted at the airport. (His first thought? *He looks like a kid!* And, at 19 years old, I guess he was!) Somehow my daddy knew from the start that one day he would give his blessing to this kid who wanted to ask his daughter for her hand in marriage.

A few months after the Wisconsin visit, it was time for me to meet Ted's family. Despite the fact that I drove Ted's newly purchased, manual transmission car with the emergency brake on, hit a tree while skiing, and had my rental skis stolen, they somehow weren't scared off. Mom and Dad Jacobson told Ted that if he didn't ask me to marry him, they would!

We had spent all or parts of about 15 days in person when we got engaged in November 1996. Christmas break gave us several weeks to spend together. We completed a workbook for engaged couples and started planning our June wedding. I did my student teaching over the winter trimester and then moved to Colorado to live with Ted's parents while working a full-time job. Ted came home on the weekends from the Air Force Academy, and our brief time together consisted of premarital counseling, shopping for wedding rings, and discussing our dreams for the future. I knew I'd be a military spouse but truly had no idea what that would involve. My ideas for the future involved teaching high school English and making a difference in the lives of teenagers by introducing them to the wonders of writing and literature. (Perhaps I took *Dead Poets' Society* a bit too seriously...)

On the morning of May 28, 1997, Ted was commissioned as a Second Lieutenant in the United States Air Force, a special ceremony prior to graduating in Falcon Stadium with the rest of his class. I remember we drove around Colorado Springs talking about how beautiful the location was. We wondered aloud if we would ever come back for one of Ted's duty assignments. I had always been in love with the state of Colorado since family vacations occasionally brought us to the mountains to camp.

We road tripped our way to Ohio, where I had my own college graduation from Cedarville College. Then it was off to Wisconsin, where we had three weeks to finalize preparations for our wedding day—almost two years exactly from the day we had met. It was a shoestring wedding to be sure; my $350 dress was the biggest expense we had.

On June 28, 1997, we said "I do" before going off "into the wild blue yonder"—the Air Force theme song provided a grand recessional as we walked (and kissed) underneath a saber arch. We celebrated with friends and family before escaping to a bed and breakfast for the first couple of nights as husband and wife.

By God's grace and some healthy boundaries, we were both virgins on our wedding day...casting rays of wonder, beauty, and, yes, awkwardness on the days and nights of our honeymoon. Getting pregnant was the farthest thing from our minds—we were newlyweds, and we meant to enjoy everything that entailed...

Chapter 2
The Birth Control Decision...Part 1

While student teaching during our engagement, I lived with a family connected with the college I attended. This allowed me to save money on room and board, as I paid my way in daily chores plus some money to help with groceries. Laurie, the wife, was a homeschooling mother of two young children and partway through a pregnancy considered high risk because she had previously experienced several miscarriages.

Though I did not realize it at the time, the months I lived with Laurie and her family influenced me greatly. After some candid conversations with Laurie, I decided to read a book on natural family planning. Ted and I discussed this method (through letters—we were still two time zones away!) and decided this "felt" right to us. It made sense and fit with our biblical worldview. I began charting my cycles, taking my temperature in the mornings and cross-checking other signs of fertility so I could learn more about my body.

Just before spring break, when I officially finished my college activities and was preparing to leave for home, a well-meaning friend in the nursing program sat me down and had a frank talk with me. Her sister had gotten pregnant on her honeymoon, and though the baby was a joy to the family, apparently the relationship between the young couple became very strained. My friend gave me information about the Depo-Provera shot, encouraging me not to pursue natural family planning because, she insisted, I would most certainly end up pregnant on our honeymoon!

I took the information home with me and talked with my doctor and my mother about it. My sweet mother and I have always had a close relationship, and though I could talk to her about almost anything, this was not necessarily an area of frank discussion in our family. The methods she and my dad had chosen for birth control seemed old fashioned and undesirable for me, and so I pursued what seemed best to me at the time.

Sadly, this was a decision I would later regret for multiple reasons. I did not research this option. Not at all. I accepted what my friend and my doctor told me as truth, and I allowed the fear of an unplanned pregnancy to direct my choices. I got my first Depo-Provera shot prior to our wedding and didn't think any more about this issue for a long while. It wasn't until about six months later that I realized I was in hormonal chaos. I weighed

30 pounds more than I had on my wedding day and experienced erratic bleeding with mood swings so alarming it's a miracle my new husband didn't up and leave me. I had three shots altogether before I decided enough was enough.

Unfortunately, my next choice wasn't much of an improvement. I listened to the doctor and switched to the birth control pill. Once again, I did not research one little bit. I had been conditioned to believe that all medical people are trustworthy and did not consider it my responsibility to examine and evaluate what I chose to allow into my body systems. I wanted "peace of mind." I wanted freedom. I wanted to control my life—and my life plans at this point most certainly did not include children.

Why not? I look back at my 22-year-old self and wonder...why was I so opposed to getting pregnant? I was married with a loving, supportive husband who had a steady, stable income. We loved Jesus and each other. We had healthy friendships and a church family that welcomed us with open arms during our one-year duty assignment in Texas. Had I gotten pregnant in those early days of marriage, the community around us would have rejoiced and helped us with the transition to parenthood. But we didn't even entertain the idea.

What was I doing that was so important that we felt we needed to put off starting a family? At the time, we desired to pay off our debts: my student loans (totaling about $15,000) and Ted's car loan. I earned $45 a day as a substitute teacher for the San Angelo school system, and nearly every cent of my little paychecks went toward our loan payments. I couldn't wait to move to our next duty station so that I could get a full-time teaching job and really make headway on paying down those loans.

But when I take an honest look at myself back then, the truth is that I wasn't even open to the idea of having children. If you had asked me why, I probably could not have given any good reasons. But in pondering the matter over the last decade or so, I've identified a couple of factors that most likely contributed to the paradigm that shaped my view of marriage and the family.

First, my own family dynamics. I grew up in a Christian home with a godly mom and dad, for whom I am extremely grateful. I attended private Christian schools from kindergarten through high school. But despite being with peers, it's entirely possible that I was sheltered even more than the average homeschooled kid would have been in the 1980's. Sex and family planning were not dinner table conversations—my only brother was four years younger than I, and such matters were kept strictly private between my mother and myself. My parents were of a generation that was not known for being frank about sensitive topics; consequently, I was given a pile of books to read on my own and encouraged to come to Mom or Dad if I had any questions (a thought that mortified me).

My parents didn't meet until they were in their late 20's. My mom had me when she was 30 years old and my brother at 34. I grew up hearing their conversations with other people about how they were happy with their "one girl and one boy," and I know they truly were grateful the Lord had blessed them with the two of us. They weren't even sure they'd be able to have another baby after me. So even though my parents never directly said as much, I somehow internalized the idea that a perfect family was a mom, dad, and two kids—ideally one girl and one boy. When I was nearing my wedding date, I briefly discussed birth control options with my mom, but I think that because of the conversation with my nursing friend from college, I had already made up my mind to get the Depo-Provera shot regardless of what Mom thought. (And honestly, I don't remember if she gave me her opinion—she likely didn't know much about Depo-Provera herself.) I made my decision based on what I thought was best for me—a selfishness I did not even realize was so deeply rooted until years later.

Aside from my upbringing, I believe the culture of Christianity in which I was immersed also inadvertently contributed to my flawed ideas about God's design for the family. In saying this, I want to clarify that I have the utmost love and respect for the churches and schools I attended growing up in Texas and during my high school years in Wisconsin. I learned so much truth in these places and really grew in my understanding of God and His Word. Just as is true with my family dynamics, there is nothing *specific* about what I was taught that made me feel and believe the way I did, but rather an overall, abstract philosophy that colored the way I viewed marriage and raising children.

You see, hardly anyone I knew had more than two or three kids in their household. And nobody really talked about the biblical view of bearing and raising children. It wasn't until I was a young mother myself that I even heard a pastor speak from the pulpit about this subject, and what he shared that day made a huge impression on me. I was not even at my usual church, but listening to this man speak about how children are a blessing, not a burden, I all of a sudden realized how *different* this message was! Never had I heard a spiritual leader discuss children in such a way, almost with a sense of awe as he shared how God had revealed much of His Father's heart to him personally as he became a father of four children of his own. In the years since, we have found ourselves in different circles with folks who acknowledge the value of children and place a high priority on parenthood, and I can't help but wonder if I simply missed these kinds of teachings in my churches and schools because of my own oblivious, self-focused tendencies or if the topic really was overlooked.

Along with this seeming omission, my Christian circles gave us constant encouragement to make our lives count, to use our gifts and talents for the Lord (an important lesson, to be sure). I never heard any of my pastors or teachers discuss the precious opportunities motherhood and fatherhood provided for shaping lives for eternity. I followed many of my Christian peers on the path to a college education for the purpose of pursuing a career that would win a paycheck as well as souls for Christ.

So here I was, still a newlywed, and definitely not ready to be a parent anytime soon. But the Depo-Provera shot had wreaked such havoc on my body and emotions that I knew I had to stop getting it. To this day I regret my decision to use birth control pills. I wish I had known then what I've learned since. I wish I had had the courage and the faith to research what I was putting into my body *on purpose*. I wish I had fully comprehended the ramifications of what the Pill could or would do, not only to my body, but also possibly to the microscopic body of a newly conceived being[2]. I can only pray that in my stubbornness and ignorance, our loving and gracious God chose to prevent any conceptions during the nearly two and a half years I willingly allowed the Depo-Provera shot or the Pill to be in my body.

---

[2] For one article on this subject, see
https://aaplog.org/birth-control-pill-abortifacient-and-contraceptive/

Chapter 3
The Early Years

We spent our first year as a married couple in the thriving metropolis of San Angelo, Texas. We found a nice little apartment and settled into married life. Ted was a willing participant in my cooking experiments (even when I accidentally omitted the yeast for our homemade pizza one night!). We jumped into music, youth, and college ministries in our local church and met a wonderful couple, Ryan and Annette, who had gotten married the same day as us. The four of us became fast friends and stay in touch to this day. We built some truly wonderful relationships with the folks in our church as well as Ted's classmates.

A year goes by quickly, and soon we were on our way to our first "real" assignment—Mountain Home AFB in Idaho! What an adventure! We spent our first anniversary in Yellowstone National Park on our way north, finally arriving at the base in what looked like the middle of absolutely nowhere. When a unit opened up, we moved into a base house and enjoyed the seemingly luxurious space compared to our previous apartment. The large backyard begged for appreciation, so we got a dog and became a "family of three." Julie (named Juliet by the family who found her and put her up for adoption) quickly became the center of attention in our home, and we loved taking her with us wherever we went on our own adventures: boating on the lake, exploring the parks, rollerblading along the flight line—the sun glinting off the wings of bombers, tankers, and jets was a sight to behold when we skated along our evening route.

We found a new church home, a tiny Baptist church in town. Their pianist had recently moved, so I gladly stepped in and played piano every Sunday morning. In the afternoons we made another trip into town so Ted and I both could practice with the worship team before the evening service.

Ted's Air Force assignment was a three-year tour, so it was time for me to get serious about a real job. Subbing had given me some good experience, but I wanted my own classroom. I interviewed for an English position at the local high school but did not receive a job offer. So I scoured the papers for any kind of job that would give me good experience plus a decent paycheck.

I saw an ad for a speech and composition teacher at a local business college, so I called and scheduled an interview. When I say "college," I'm talking a couple of storefront windows along Main Street. The couple who founded the school seemed very kind and very eager to put me to work. I was hired for the fall semester to teach speech, American literature, and composition. But they also needed some summer instructors, and so I found myself immediately working as a word processing and computer skills instructor.

The summer courses met during the day, but when fall came, the classes I was to teach would be in the evenings. This is because the small student population consisted mostly of adults working toward an associate's degree, some stay-at-home moms who wanted to further their education and other adults who had full-time jobs during the day. My classes met Monday through Thursday evenings, and living on base meant I would be commuting into the tiny town of Mountain Home right about dinner time.

As the school year start date approached, I got a phone call from the district asking me if I would be willing to interview for a new position at the high school. They remembered me from the previous interview and requested specifically that I come back. Since my goal was to get hired as an English teacher at that school, I figured it was worth checking into.

The school had received funding for a Career Center Coordinator. They had already set aside a room and resources; the area needed to be organized, and they wanted someone to staff it full-time. I was excited by the possibilities; I would be working with the guidance counselors as well as high school students. Oh, joy! Finally I would get to work with teens! Plus, a foot in the door for a future teaching job!

I went home and told Ted my wonderful news. I'm not even sure we really discussed it—it was a done deal in my mind. The fact that I would work an eight-hour job in town during the day, drive home for a quick dinner, then drive back into town to teach night classes...well, that couldn't be helped. I was going to get some incredible experience, and besides, this was ministry! I was helping people!

Ted was supportive; he always has supported my wild ideas. But as the school year went on, we both realized that this was not an ideal situation. I loved my jobs and found great fulfillment in working through the various challenges each presented. I loved my students in the night classes (all of whom were older than I!), and I loved everything about the people as well as the opportunities I had in my daytime job at the high school career center. But working two jobs while commuting back and forth twice a day took a toll. Shifting my night class schedule during the spring semester to two evenings a week instead of four did help, but the burnout and long hours plus prep work on the weekends did not do great things for my relationship with my husband.

As we headed toward summer, I was offered a full-time teaching job at the high school, which I gladly accepted. I gave my notice at the business school—no way was I going to continue to teach night classes. It had been a long, hard year, but the way I saw it, the long days and hard work had been worth it: I had received valuable experience, and I had achieved my goal of getting the position I wanted. Definitely worth it. Right?

Looking back, I realize it was not, in fact, "worth it." I did not learn until much later exactly what a toll my workaholic schedule had taken on my husband and on my marriage. We attended a marriage conference along with other couples in our church, and during our talks together that weekend, things came out that hit me to the core. I realized how utterly selfish I had been during that year, pursuing my goals and desires above all else. We were both young and inexperienced in many ways, and while there were hurts on both sides, I take responsibility for much of it. If I had focused on my marriage and given it proper priority, I believe we could have avoided many mistakes and a lot of pain.

But God is so gracious! His love and mercy protected us from failures that could have led us down a path with a much different ending. I am grateful that He tenderly woos us back to Him. You see, I was so busy doing things "for God" (I thought) that I neglected my biggest gift FROM God: my husband. I pursued my career nearly at the expense of my marriage. I put ministry activities in higher priority than the one person to whom I am called to minister all the days of my life, until death do us part. And I certainly did not leave room for God to do anything different than what I had written on the planner of my own life.

In October 1999, that all changed. God has a way of getting our attention, doesn't He?

Chapter 4
Charis Noelle

ancreatic cancer. Jim Jacobson—Ted's dad, my gentle, kind, wise and wise-acre father-in-law— was the last person we ever thought would battle such a disease. His healthy lifestyle made him an unlikely candidate for such a thing, but here we were, reeling as a family from the news that the doctors had confirmed cancer in his body and given him a year to live.

Stubborn man that he was, Jim refused to diminish his quality of life by undergoing chemotherapy or radiation. He ramped up his research and focused on a natural approach to support his body during this time. I think most of us were in denial during the early days following the diagnosis. Surely Jim of all people had a good chance of beating this disease. His vitamin and supplement regimen along with regular exercise and healthy eating habits—surely he would be an overcomer.

But the whole situation gave me pause. A little niggling thought in the back of my mind grew to disturbing proportions. All of a sudden I was aware of an overwhelming idea: what if our decision to delay starting a family had been rooted in selfishness? What if all this time our ideas about financial responsibility and the pursuit of our careers were just a means of controlling our own lives?

What if... *what if* these decisions meant we had deprived Jim of the privilege and opportunity of meeting a grandchild here on earth?

All of a sudden I began thinking—*really* thinking—about this whole family planning issue. I saw everything from a completely different perspective. Both Ted and I are firstborns; neither of our younger brothers were married at this time. If we were to have a baby, it would be the first grandchild on both sides of our family.

I fell under the conviction of the Holy Spirit and wept. I saw more clearly how my selfishness over the past couple of years had not only affected my own life and marriage, but also the lives of other people I loved. It had never occurred to me that our own little family dynamics would have such ripple effects on other people. I realize not everyone will agree with the idea that one's personal family decisions ought also to be considerate of other people, but when I look through Scripture and see the value that God places on the entire family, I can't help but come to the conclusion that our lives, our decisions, are not simply for US but first of all for the glory of the God who created us and second for the benefit of those around us whom we have the privilege of loving and serving.

And so I would say our journey as a family begins with *grace*; looking back, I see how very selfish I was in wanting to have my own agenda met before starting a family. I never even asked God to direct us in this matter! Instead I was pursuing a career and heavily involved in ministry activities—all good things, but since my other priorities were out of whack, these pursuits turned out to be idols, distractions from what God really wanted for me as a woman and for Ted and me as a couple. Yielding control of our family situation was the first step in repenting, and God abundantly poured out His grace accordingly.

Ted and I discussed this during the fall as he prepared for a deployment over the holidays. We agreed that I would stop taking birth control pills during this time of separation and allow God to do whatever He desired with our family.

And so it was that Charis was knit in my womb— likely moments after Ted returned from his deployment to Turkey! How exciting, thrilling, and yes, just a bit terrifying to see that positive pregnancy test. (I had no idea I would take so many pregnancy tests over the course of time!) We were so excited to share our news not only with our dear family and friends but also anyone else who would listen. We picked out a name, Charis Noelle, when I was only eight weeks pregnant, long before we knew our baby's gender. Her name was the only one we didn't keep secret throughout the whole pregnancy; we announced it to the world as soon as the ultrasound revealed our firstborn was a girl!

Charis—Greek for grace.

Noelle—the birthday of the Lord, the advent of Grace.

I have always loved our daughter's name, and I cherish the meaning. I will never, ever get over God's amazing grace, first poured out on us at Calvary—that Jesus, our holy, precious Lord, would allow ignorant, sinful, brutal humans to have their way with Him, marring His body but not His will...that He would cry, "Father, forgive them, for they know not what they do." I hope we never get over the marvelous miracle that is our salvation!

Our grace story isn't a one-time event. "For from his fullness we have all received grace upon grace. For the law was given through Moses; grace and truth came through Jesus Christ" (John 1:16-17). Being a mother has been one of the best lessons in grace I could have asked for (though I'm not sure I asked for it!). Not only have I learned over the years to extend grace to others— a difficult thing for me, a person who values justice and leans toward the "eye for an eye" approach more often than not—but also to extend grace to myself, for I am my own worst critic and have a hard time when I don't meet the high expectations I set for myself. And forgiving myself when I become aware of my poor choices and failings continues to be a struggle, even as I gratefully acknowledge the Lord's forgiveness and mercy to me on a daily basis.

How I thank God for sending us our firstborn, a precious baby girl who has taught us so much as we've stumbled through this parenting process. What a joy it was to share with our parents the news that we were expecting their first grandchild! In typical fashion, Jim's response reflected his good humor and intuitiveness. He apparently was not surprised by the news, though we hadn't told anyone about our decision to stop any form of birth control. He said Rhonda (Ted's mom) had wondered aloud one day when Ted and I might start a family, and he quipped, "I'm guessing it will be about 9 months after Ted returns from his deployment!" And he was right!

Ted and I drove to Denver in March of 2000 to spend time with his folks, and then we all met in Butte, Montana, for his grandparents' fiftieth wedding anniversary celebration in June. We made plans for Ted to go to Colorado for a hunting trip with his dad in the fall, and since my due date was in October, we decided Thanksgiving would be a reasonable time for us to make another trip to introduce baby Charis to her grand-parents.

But God had other plans. On October 15, 2000, Ted and I were at church in Mountain Home, Idaho, when a phone call came through to the church office. This was in the pre-historic days before smart phones, and when a church leader came looking for Ted to tell him he had a long-distance phone call, our hearts filled with dread. We were so sure we would get to see Jim at least one more time—because he simply had to meet his first grand-child. But it was not to be—not as we imagined it. Jim

29

had died peacefully at home, stepping into the arms of his Savior while Charis was still squirming in close quarters inside my womb. By God's mercy, though we usually called Mom and Dad Jacobson every Sunday, for some reason that week we had called Saturday instead. What a blessing to be able to talk with him one last time, though of course we did not realize it to be the last until afterward.

Ted flew to Colorado to be with his family and plan the memorial service, held two days later. I longed to be with him during this time, to grieve in person with those I love and pay respects to my father-in-law, a true gift from the Lord—it is in large part because of his life and example that my husband is the amazing, wonderful man that he is. But with my due date being October 20, there was no way I would be allowed to step foot onto an airplane. I did my grieving and praying at home.

The evening of the memorial service, October 17, I spoke with Ted on the phone. I didn't have definite signs of impending labor, but something was "different," enough so that my mother-in-law decided to get Ted on an airplane immediately so he could come home and be with his wife. Little did any of us know how important that decision turned out to be. It was hard for Ted to leave his family in Colorado, knowing he would not be there to help carry his father's casket to the grave site in Wyoming. But my labor pains started coming not even 2 hours after Ted arrived home. It was not a quick or easy labor—it was a long day for me, as I'm sure it was for Ted's mom and his brother Joel and all those who drove from Colorado to Wyoming to lay Jim's body to rest. But at the end of it all, with much labor and love and effort and sweat and tears, Charis arrived on the scene, a beautiful, writhing baby girl, a true gift of grace to the Jacobson family, a Hello from God even as we were saying Goodbye. *Sunrise, sunset.*

I absolutely have no doubt that Grandpa J had a front row seat from heaven, watching his granddaughter enter the world! Oh, how we wish he could have held Charis in his arms. Jim Jacobson loved babies! It still makes my heart sad that he was never able to hold and play with any of our kids here on earth.

I embraced the role of stay-at-home mother, shedding some tears the day Charis turned six weeks old. For awhile during my pregnancy, I had entertained the idea of teaching full-time one more year. But ultimately, I decided I'd rather just stay home—and my relieved husband heartily agreed. I was touched that he had been prepared to support me if I had chosen to keep my full-time job, even though he really wanted me to stay home and enjoy being a mama full-time. Once we were in the throes of parenthood, it was clear to us both just how difficult it can be "simply" to feed, clothe, and care for a wee human being!

Having Charis filled our lives with joy during what otherwise would have been a tremendously difficult time after Ted's dad passed. Undoubtedly Rhonda had a much more challenging transition, having lost the love of her life after 27 years of marriage. But the sleepless nights and steep learning curve that every parent must endure took every ounce of energy and awareness we could muster. Though the week had been a roller coaster of emotions for us, we found ourselves thanking the Lord for blessing us with the precious gift of life for such a time as this. We took every opportunity to share time with Rhonda and Joel, hosting them along with Ted's sister and her fiancé for Thanksgiving; meeting in Montana for Christmas with the Butte family; flying to Colorado in February 2001 to surprise Mom for her fiftieth birthday.

As spring came, Ted prepared for another short deployment. I flew with Charis to visit my family in Wisconsin. She was getting to be quite the seasoned little traveler! I loved showing her off. This motherhood thing was suiting me well, I thought. We had had a rough start with nursing, but I gritted my teeth through the pain and made it to the other side after about six weeks.

Having been a one-car family for our entire stint in Idaho, we decided as our moving date approached that it was time to upgrade. I was thrilled with the new-to-us Subaru Outback that seated us much more comfortably than squeezing two adults and a car seat into Ted's two-door Saturn! Of course we kept his car—it had been paid off shortly after Charis was born, just like my school loans, allowing us to finance a second car.

In the heat of July 2001, we said goodbye to dear friends in Idaho and began the long drive to our next duty assignment at Wright-Patterson AFB in Dayton, Ohio. Our dog Julie and nine-month-old Charis provided each vehicle with a special soundtrack as we made our way across America!

Chapter 5
Tobin Michael

House hunting in the Dayton area had been exciting, but now that we were waiting to close on the home we had purchased, spending the long days in the vintage TLF (Temporary Lodging Facilities) was tedious, to put it mildly. Ted had already begun his new job, and there was not much for me to do besides take Charis out for a walk to get away from our tiny room with nasty carpet which left black smudges on her pudgy little knees and feet as she crawled and scooted across the floor.

At least the TLF was close to the commissary and the BX (base exchange), not to mention a park, so when it was too hot to be exploring the far reaches of the Kittyhawk Center, we did our grocery shopping for the day and wandered around the furniture and garden areas of the BX, dreaming of the day we would finally move into our own house.

It wasn't too long after settling into this new routine that felt I needed to make a particular purchase: a home pregnancy test. I was still nursing Charis, but my monthly cycle had returned the month before yet did not show up the next month. I wondered if my body was going to take some time to adjust, but I had enough of a niggling suspicion that I finally decided to just buy a test and put my mind at ease. I knew a pregnancy was a possibility—the doctor in Idaho had put me on the "mini-pill" after my post-partum check-up six weeks after Charis's birth. However, I began to feel very uncomfortable about using the pills at all, and with Ted's full awareness, I stopped.

So it wasn't entirely shocking when I saw the two lines appear on the pregnancy test. I felt a thumping in my chest, a shortness of breath, as I took it all in and did some quick calculating. Our babies would be...18 months apart?! Oh. Oh, my. Deep breaths. *OK, this can actually be a good thing. Charis can have a baby sister! They can share clothes, maybe a room, and they'll be best friends!* I never had a sister, and I was always a bit sad that my brother and I didn't grow very close until after I moved out of the house. I figured the age difference as well as gender contributed in part, and I hoped that our babies would be closer while growing up.

I spent a good bit of time plotting and scheming how to tell Ted the news. Clearly I had much more time on my hands in those days, because I created an elaborate game board with cards to draw depending on what space we landed. After dinner, when we put Charis to bed, there was not a lot we could do, since the TLF was little more than a hotel room with a kitchenette and a partition to close off the tiny bedroom. With Charis sleeping in the playpen in the main area, we were stuck in our bedroom from early evening until the next morning. (Obviously this was conducive to conceiving Charis's sibling!) On this particular evening, I was nearly bursting but managed to keep quiet so my "game plan" could work itself out. And so it was that eventually we hit the "tell your partner a secret" card, and since Ted was stumped, I offered to share a secret instead! He was surprised but pleased. We were more eager than ever to move into our own home and receive our household goods.

The day before Move-In, I needed to do a bit of shopping. As I stood in line at the BX, I stared in disbelief as the news on the checkout TV screens showed images that couldn't be real—and yet the footage was not from a movie. It was the morning of September 11, 2001. I watched dumbfounded along with the other customers. An airplane had crashed into one of the Twin Towers in New York City. I finished my transaction and hurried through my shopping at the next stop. By the time I got to that checkout line, the news was showing the second tower's fate. Choking back sobs and panic, I fairly ran back to our TLF unit with Charis in her stroller. I had to get a hold of my husband. Our parents were calling me, wanting to make sure we were all right, and I had no idea what was going on. Once I heard Ted's voice on the phone, I was somewhat reassured, but as he could not leave work, I put Charis in bed for a nap (having no idea whether she slept or not) and watched news coverage the rest of the day. For those who don't remember 9/11, it's hard to describe the emotions of that day. We thought the world might be coming to an end.

Ted was cleared to go forward with our moving day on September 12. It was surreal, doing something that felt so permanent when we had no idea what our world would look like in the coming days. But over the weeks that followed, the nation slowly let out its collective breath, and we dared to believe that just maybe we could live again. I will never forget the U.S. flags that waved from almost every front porch and on vehicles, the strains of "God Bless the USA" that played in restaurants and grocery stores, and the feeling that strangers wearing patriotic shirts were actually long-lost friends. The sense of unity held us together...for awhile anyway. It was beautiful while it lasted.

Life went on in our little home. We learned that Charis would actually have a baby brother instead of a sister, so I began scouring baby name books looking for an unusual boy name that wouldn't be all chopped up in a nickname. While I was living with Laurie's family during my student teaching days, I learned that they chose their baby names with an E-L in them. *El* is Hebrew for God. I liked that idea. In fact, I liked the idea of choosing names deliberately based on their meaning. Laurie reminded me that the Bible is full of examples of names with specific meaning, even names that were changed because of special circumstances or promises. Ted and I really appreciated the concept of praying over a name and then praying for its meaning to be made manifest in a special way in that child's life. We felt perhaps first names with E-L might be a bit limiting, since we wanted unique names, but almost all of our children's middle names do have E-L in them (all but one—that chapter comes later!).

I finally found a first name with a meaning that stood out to me: "The Lord is great." In the post-9/11 days, I worried and wondered about bringing a baby into such a world as ours. But God knew about the terrorist acts long before they happened, just as He knew and purposed for my son to exist at just this time. I loved the idea that his name would remind me no matter what happens, my God is in control—He is infinitely greater than anything that may rise up against us. He is more powerful than circumstances that seem to be spinning us out of control.

So I found a name whose meaning I greatly appreciated. However, I was not crazy about the Hebrew name Tobias, so I chose a derivation of it: Tobin. And when I read the meaning for Michael ("Who is like the Lord?"), I felt that together, Tobin Michael had a powerful ring.

The Lord is great! Who is like the Lord?!

We shared the name with our parents but no one else. On April 13, 2002, Tobin Michael was born in the quiet, peaceful hours of the night. His cord was wrapped around his neck, but some quick actions by our labor and delivery team allowed me to hold him before long. The six-hour labor and delivery process was much less strenuous than had been my first experience, and I walked with a tiny Tobin from the delivery room to our hospital room, where we delighted in holding and getting to know our firstborn son. We were immediately in love with this tiny, wrinkled baby boy, with his fuzzy blonde hair and hands that seemed disproportionately large compared to his 7-pound, 10-ounce little body, hands that reflected generations of hard-working men.

He looked so much like his daddy...AND like his Grandpa J.

Chapter 6
Arden Daniel

My days and my heart were full. Having two children under two was both a total delight and an exercise in patience. Before Tobin was born, when I tucked Charis in at night, I remember holding her close, praying over her, and feeling my heart would simply burst with the love I had for this one little person. I wondered how in the world I could ever love another child the way I loved her. And now I knew.

I was in full scrapbooking mode, snapping photos of the cutest kids on the planet and mounting them on elaborately decorated pages, a hobby which went well with my home business at the time. We had settled happily into our Ohio life, finding another good church and developing the kind of friendships so necessary to continual growth. We had also found a good home for our sweet dog Julie, who unfortunately was not as good with our kids as she was with other people's kids. A military family with three children gladly took her in, and though it was bittersweet saying goodbye to our fur baby, it was for the best—my hands were full, and I could not give our energetic pooch the time and attention she needed.

I found a helpful book, *Taking Charge of Your Fertility* by Toni Weschler, and had decided (along with Ted, who patiently listened to me process the information) that I was no longer willing to use chemical birth control. I remembered our decision prior to marriage to use natural family planning, and I felt tinges of regret that I had allowed myself to go in a different direction. TCOYF, as this book is known, seemed a bit easier to understand and implement than the NFP book I had read during our engagement. I felt this was something I could actually do.

Thus began a long season of charting. I quickly found patterns in my body's cycles and began to feel much more comfortable with the whole method. Even better, I felt a tremendous sense of peace. This felt right to me—I no longer worried about harming my body or (even unintentionally) causing a hostile environment within my womb that might result in the killing of a newly conceived child.

There came a night when we...tested the limits, shall we say...of the "safe" period. We were fully aware that there was a possibility of conception, and while we weren't necessarily feeling ready for a third child, clearly we didn't let that stop us.

A couple of weeks later, my cycle started. Whew! I thought nothing more about it. But just a couple of weeks after that, I noticed something on my charts: my temperature had gone up (as is typical during that time of a woman's cycle), but instead of coming back down to normal, it stayed up. Uh oh. Incubation!

I fretted. How could I be pregnant?! Tobin was just nine months old! I was barely handling two small children. How would we manage another baby?!

Ted had to get his wisdom teeth removed, and I was to drive him to and from the base medical center. While Ted was in surgery, I slipped over to the Women's Health Clinic to take a pregnancy test so I could schedule my first prenatal visit. The conversation went something like this:

"Hello, how may we help you?"

"Hi, um, I'm pretty sure I'm pregnant, so I guess I need to get the test to confirm so that we can schedule the orientation and whatnot..."

"OK, ma'am, what was the date of your last menstrual period?"

"Two weeks ago."

A blank stare.

"But I know my body! I've been charting! My temperature has stayed up for 18 days, so clearly I'm pregnant!"

"Um...well, ma'am, we can't give you a pregnancy test until you're two weeks late..."

"So...what if I take my own test at home and it's positive?"

"Oh, well, then you can make an appointment and come in!"

Sigh. I shuffled back to the waiting area and met my rather drugged up husband. I drove us home, stopping to get a pregnancy test along the way. I wanted confirmation of what I knew intuitively to be true: I was, indeed, pregnant with our third child.

Unlike the first two positive tests, I have to confess that this time around, I cried out of exhaustion instead of happiness. I told my husband the news as he sat foggy-headed on our living room couch, with gauze still stuffed in his mouth. He was quiet for a minute, and then he said around the cotton, "Well, I guess we're going to need to get a minivan."

Indeed.

It was nearing spring of 2003, and the war in Iraq had begun. Ted was deployed to NORAD in Colorado Springs for an indefinite amount of time. With prenatal appointments I needed to attend on my calendar, it wasn't practical for the kids and me to pack up and "move" to Colorado with Ted, but I did make a couple of cross-country trips along with my potty-training toddler and an almost one-year-old Tobin. Right before our first big road trip, I got a call from one of the OBs regarding my blood test results. It showed I had an elevated risk for our child to have Down syndrome. The doctor wanted me to come in immediately for an amniocentesis. When I told her that I was preparing to leave town for a few weeks, she assured me I could take care of things when we returned.

Take care of things? What things? And how exactly does one "take care of" something like this?

I was stunned. I had had two healthy pregnancies and two healthy children. And now...now what? There was nothing to do but pray and wait. I knew very little about Down syndrome or how having a baby with this condition might affect the rest of our family. I struggled to make sense of everything while at the same time resigning myself to not having any answers for several weeks.

During our time in Colorado, we stayed at Rhonda's house and spent time with Ted during his off days. While he worked, I kept the kids from killing themselves or each other and did a lot of praying in the early mornings before they were awake. One morning, as I was again crying out to the Lord, anxious and uncertain about the child in my womb, I felt Him very distinctly breathe assurance and peace into my soul. As surely as if I had heard an audible voice, I knew God had a special, unique purpose for the baby growing inside of me. I know this is true for every single child that is born—but there was a reason the Lord pressed this on my heart, a special calling He had on the life of this soul He had created. I had no other definite information, but a growing confidence replaced the anxiety in my spirit. The Lord had told me this child would serve His kingdom in a special way. And for now, that was enough.

Upon returning home to Ohio, I met with a different doctor who talked me through the blood test results and what they might or might not mean. When he heard I had planned to get an amniocentesis, he asked me why. I was stumped. Well, I was told to do so, wasn't I? Once again, I had not done any research. I did not even know what an amniocentesis was, let alone why I supposedly should get one!

This doctor was so gentle and kind. He asked me what we would do if we discovered our baby did have Down syndrome. I told him we would love our child and research as much as possible so that we could be better prepared to care for him or her. Since I was clearly not of a mind to abort my baby, the doctor urged me to get a diagnostic ultrasound rather than an amniocentesis. And so we did. We learned that our baby boy was perfectly healthy. A sense of relief washed over me when the doctor assured me our third child most likely did not have a chromosome abnormality. And why not? I knew no better. Little did I know we would experience a much different diagnostic ultrasound later in our parenting journey.

Ted finished his deployment as well as five weeks of Squadron Officer School in time to return home for the Baby Countdown. We had decided on this little boy's name but did not share it with anyone (not even our parents) until after he was born, a tradition that would continue with the rest of our children. Based on what I felt the Lord had pressed on my heart regarding this child, I chose the name Arden, derived from the Latin word for "fervent, passionate, on fire." I wanted Daniel (Hebrew: God is my judge) to be his middle name, because the prophet Daniel in the Bible is a man of highest integrity, a man who passionately stood for what was right despite being in a completely pagan culture. My prayer was for this child to grow into a man with fervent faith, passionate about the Lord our God and ready to stand firm in his convictions.

Arden's due date was October 17. I had hoped he would come a bit early and be born on the fifteenth, the anniversary of his grandpa's heaven-going. Instead, the boy took his sweet time and arrived a day late...which happened to be his big sister's third birthday.

Three babies in three years. Who would have thought?!

Chapter 7
Aliana Elizabeth

We spent 2004 – 2005 in Maryland while Ted got his Master's degree from the Joint Military Intelligence College at Bolling AFB, D.C. Our follow-on assignment took us to Las Vegas, Nevada, where we would spend the next four years (living in three different houses, but that's another story).

It was four days before Christmas 2005 when I took the home pregnancy test and passed. I was so excited...I had felt for awhile that we were to have at least one more child. However, I was a little nervous about breaking the news to Ted, who had mentioned on more than one occasion that he was content with our three children, and, having followed in the footsteps of both his grandpa and his dad, was thrilled by having a girl and then two boys. I needn't have worried; Ted responded happily that evening when the children were in bed and I gave him a stamped "bundle of joy" and a typed copy of my journaled thoughts from recent days.

We began making plans. Should we find a bigger house? Ted wondered. Absolutely not! I told him I felt God had led us to this house, and if He was giving us another child, we would certainly find a place for a new baby! The boys already shared a room, so we decided that the baby could move into Charis's room after the sleeping-through-the-night thing fell into place.

One thing seemed all but certain. Since early in 2005, Charis had been praying for a baby sister. When she first asked me if she could get a baby sister, I smiled and told her that she would need to ask God if that's what He wanted for our family. "Let's just pray about it," I said. "We'll see what God wants for us. If He wants you to have a baby sister, He'll send her in His perfect time." Although I had not heard Charis specifically praying for this in a few months, as Ted had been doing special bedtime prayers with her recently, Ted mentioned that Charis was still praying about a baby sister. We chuckled and decided this baby must be a girl.

About a week and a half later I experienced my first instance of spotting. It was very light, but since I had never had any spotting or bleeding at all during my other pregnancies, I was immediately concerned. I spent a good hour on the internet looking for answers. (Isn't that how we all get medical advice these days?!) I was reassured when I learned that spotting is quite common. I didn't think much about it when the spotting disappeared after a few hours.

A few days later, more spotting. A few days later, cramps. The spotting was light, the cramps were mildly uncomfortable, and more reading on the internet convinced me that all of this was very common, probably about as common as morning sickness, which I had never really endured. I noted the signs to watch for in case something really was wrong, and I continued on with life, making mental changes in preparation for another addition to our family by the end of summer.

We'll need a new car seat.

Where will this baby sleep?! Maybe in our closet...

I'll need to get our baby swing back from Page.

How in the world will I manage four children?!

My mom arrived in town to spend some time with us and help with the kids when I left for a brief training event in Memphis. It seemed my spotting was getting more and more frequent, but as it was still very light, I didn't really know if it was worth worrying about. I decided if things didn't improve, I would get checked out after I returned home.

We shared our pregnancy news with Mom the night she arrived, after the children had gone to bed. She was as delighted as we knew she would be. Though I had hoped to tell the children our exciting news as soon as possible after my mother knew, the next two evenings were a whirlwind of activity, and we never had the opportunity to sit down with them to make an announcement. Now I know that was divine intervention.

During my trip to Memphis I talked with a friend who had experienced a miscarriage. I mentioned my concern about the spotting, and she reassured me that she had bled quite a bit when she was pregnant with her first daughter but everything turned out fine. I put it out of my mind, since the spotting was still overall quite light and I wasn't having any more cramps.

The day I flew home, however, I noticed more bleeding. I just wanted to get home and rest. I had run on the treadmill at the hotel before I left that morning; perhaps the exercising had caused more bleeding. I wasn't sure, though, since I had been running for several months, and there were many times I ran even after knowing I was pregnant and nothing had happened. At home Mom encouraged me to go to bed and rest, then see how things were in the morning. She was concerned enough to tell me that if nothing had changed overnight, she thought I should go to the hospital to get checked out.

I was exhausted from my trip and slept soundly. I do remember a vivid dream, though, proving I must have been worried about the whole situation. I dreamed I was at the hospital having an ultrasound. The doctor was telling me I had miscarried a child but there were twins and one of them was still alive. I awoke immediately after this dream. I prepared to shower and discovered the spotting had become outright bleeding. I showered as quickly as I could, crying the whole time.

The day was incongruously sunny. As Ted drove us in silence to the hospital, my mind latched onto a name for our baby. I don't know why—we weren't even

49

planning to consider names until we knew for sure whether we were having a boy or a girl. But my heart told me this baby was a girl, and the name Aliana Elizabeth sprang to my mind. I didn't dwell on this too much but tucked it away, choosing instead to focus my thoughts on praying for God's will to be done and for strength to endure whatever lay ahead.

The emergency room was fairly quiet. I cried as I told the nurse what was going on, and she ushered us back to a bed with a curtain around it. Since it was Sunday, we had to wait for the on-call ultrasound technician to be called in. During the interminable waiting, I made a conscious decision to bless the name of the Lord no matter what the outcome was to be.

The tech arrived, wheeled me into another room, and began the ultrasound. She was very kind, with a soft, quiet voice. She didn't say much during the process, and I lay on the bed staring at the cracks in the ceiling, trying to ignore the discomfort.

When the ultrasound was finished and the data entered, the woman sat back with a small sigh. "Technically I'm not supposed to say anything," she said, staring at the computer screen. Then she turned to look at me. "But you pretty much knew already..."

I nodded, a lump in my throat. There was nothing to say, and I wouldn't have been able to speak even if I needed to.

The good news, she said, was that the pregnancy looked to be normal, not tubal. She continued by saying the results would be sent to the lab, and then the doctor would notify Ted and me and speak with us further. She left to get Ted for me, and I lay waiting and praying.

You give and take away...Lord, blessed be Your name...

Ted and I had some quiet moments together in the ultrasound room before the tech came back to wheel me back to our cubicle. The delays were all the more unbearable at this point, since we knew what had happened, and there was nothing more to be done but sit around waiting to be released.

Finally the doctor came to inform us of what we already knew. Though he seemed sympathetic, he irked me when he referred to me likely passing more "products of conception." *It's a baby,* I wanted to shout. *I've lost my baby, not a fetus, not a product of conception.* By this point our baby would have been about the size of a grain of rice. Fingers and toes were forming, bones were developing. Though I have no physical evidence to prove the gender, in my heart I know I was carrying a girl, just as I knew Charis was a girl when I was eight weeks pregnant with her. We named her Charis Noelle at that point, figuring we could come up with a boy name later just in case, but we never did.

I don't remember much about the ride home, but I do remember falling into bed for a three-hour nap, mercifully dreamless. Waking from my nap was one of the most difficult times of this whole ordeal for me, because I had to go through everything all over again in my head, reminding myself that I was no longer pregnant. It all seemed so surreal. That didn't really happen. It couldn't have. I've wanted this baby for a long time. Charis prayed for this baby for almost a year. Why did God seemingly answer our prayers, only to take it back after two short months? I found comfort in the thought that Ted's dad, our baby's Grandpa J, would get to meet this little one before the rest of the family did.

We announced our loss via email to a few friends and family members who already knew of our pregnancy, and I was overwhelmed by the response. Over the next few days I could feel the prayers of loved ones—they truly upheld me and gave me strength. Not only that, I was amazed at how many women confided to me about their own experience of pregnancy loss. Only once had I ever heard from someone about this topic. I thought it was dreadful that so many women stuffed their feelings for years, even a lifetime, never speaking of lost little ones. I resolved to be willing to share my experience any time it would bring someone encouragement or comfort

One morning some days after losing our baby, I went for an early run. As I turned west, I could see the mountains rising in a purple haze, dusted with snow on top. The sight took my breath away, and I thought of Psalm 121:1-2, "I lift up my eyes to the hills—where does my help come from? My help comes from the Lord, the Maker of heaven and earth." I felt in a tangible way the presence of my Almighty God, Creator of all life, including the short-lived earthly life of our little one. I drank in the morning air, praising God for Who He is and all He has done. After awhile, I remembered the name I had thought of for our baby as we made that dreadful drive to the emergency room.

Aliana Elizabeth. Yes, I knew in my heart that was to be her name. Aliana, a name I had heard from a godly mother I met briefly in a restaurant in Maryland. When I asked her what her daughter's name meant, she told me, "Light bearer, or giver of light." Elizabeth: God's oath.

Aliana, you never had the opportunity to personally give light to others while you were here, but it is my prayer that through the pain and sadness of losing you, your daddy and I can somehow bring light to others, the Light of the world Who knows and understands our pain. Aliana Elizabeth, God never promised me a perfect pregnancy, or even a healthy newborn baby. But the promises He has given me are even more precious, for they are eternal.

I will see you someday, little one.

Chapter 8
Kenna Joelle

Charis didn't know about the loss of our baby until years later, but for some reason she stopped asking for a baby sister. I was grateful. I never knew when emotions would burst out of me during unexpected provocation (such as Sanctity of Life Sunday at church the week after the miscarriage happened). As time went on, life seemed to get back to "normal," but I wasn't sure I'd ever really be normal again. How could losing such a tiny little being hurt so badly?

I felt a strange, unexpected sense of compassion for women who have had an abortion. I wondered if they felt the same internal, emotional pain that I felt, maybe even more so, since their choices resulted in the void in their womb. I pondered being pro-life, a stance which meant holding signs and praying in strategic places back when I was in high school and college. But in truth, I was learning to live out my pro-life convictions in a way that looked much different than pithy bumper stickers or pointed billboards. Though my circumstances were much, much different, I felt that, if given the opportunity to speak or pray with a woman who has experienced the violence of abortion, just maybe I would be more compassionate, more empathetic, for the turmoil she would undoubtedly feel simply for having gone through my own experience of painful loss.

Physically, I was doing just fine. Emotionally, I still had my moments. The pain didn't just go away simply because I recognized God is good all the time. Mentally, I felt stronger than I could have expected, having been through great sadness and finding myself becoming more keenly aware of God's presence, listening to His Word speak to me, and following the Holy Spirit more closely.

Our life continued. We did home school activities every morning, got together with friends, attended church events, served in our places of ministry, ate, drank, slept, laughed, and loved. My routine, my beliefs, my values—those were the same. It was my heart and mind that were different. I now understood more fully the meaning of grief and sadness, the gut-wrenching pain of losing someone dear, a precious, God-created life. At the same time, I could also more fully appreciate God's hand in every aspect of my life. I learned it's not enough to sing glib praise songs, to say I believe God has a plan for me and those I love. What truly matters is that God is God, worthy of praise whether I feel like praising Him or not. He deserves my praise—He deserved it before I even knew Him, simply because of Who He is. Even if He did absolutely nothing for me, He is still worthy to be praised. But oh, thank you, Jesus, you did everything for me! For us!

I was still charting, and we had agreed to carefully avoid getting pregnant. I wasn't sure my heart could take it. Then in June my cycle was much shorter than usual. And Charis began asking, once again, if she could have a baby sister. We went through the same conversations we had had months previously.

"Well, honey, we don't know what God wants for our family. We can pray and ask Him!"

One day Charis looked right at me and responded in as firm a voice as a five-year-old could muster: "I HAVE been praying, and I think God wants us to have another baby!"

I took the pregnancy test the next day. Turns out Charis was right.

I prayed and pondered much during the early days of this pregnancy. I finally stopped expecting to see blood and dared to believe this baby would be one I would hold in my arms someday. I realized God had changed my heart tremendously over the course of this journey; I was starting to think we should stop even trying to control whether or not we conceived a child. (Some might argue we weren't doing a very good job of that anyway! But I would point to the three-and-a-half-year age gap between babies 3 and 4 as evidence that the fertility awareness method can, indeed, work!)

Of course this baby was a girl. We knew that from the beginning, since Charis had been praying for a sister! By now hunting for the right baby name was more like a quest. We wanted two syllables for both first and middle names, with E-L in the middle name and a first name that was both pleasing to the ear as well as unique. Kenna, Scottish for "to tell or make known," went beautifully with Joelle, and when we fit both names together, the meaning was significant. We prayed our daughter would "tell or make known that Jehovah is God."

With a due date of March 12, 2007, Ted's six-month deployment to Tampa would span my third trimester and the first three months of our baby's life. But it couldn't be helped; active duty personnel go where and when they are needed. We felt thankful for the asthma diagnosis that allowed Ted to continue serving on active duty but prevented him from deploying outside the contiguous 48 states. We planned for the kids and me to fly from Vegas to Tampa for the holidays, and then Ted would fly home over a couple of three-day weekends. He would be allowed to come home for the birth as well. As far as deployments go, we felt we got off fairly easy!

The pregnancy progressed uneventfully. We had a beautiful time together in Florida, spending Christmas with our little family in Ted's two-bedroom apartment (which later housed another military member). We took the kids to the Magic Kingdom and Dinosaur World and made some precious memories before returning to Nevada.

We were two weeks away from Kenna's due date when the first contractions hit me. I stayed at home for some hours as they came and went, but by 3 a.m. it was clear I needed to get to the hospital. Our baby birth plans went into high gear; one friend came to stay at the house with the sleeping children while another drove me to the hospital at Nellis AFB. The actual moment Kenna was born, Ted was boarding his plane to come home, having gotten my phone call just as he was waking up for the day in Tampa. Kenna stormed into the world on her own terms, arriving three hours after we drove away from the house. She was my first all-natural delivery, and I was thankful for her tiny 6-pound, 5-ounce little body, since I was not entirely prepared to forego the epidural!

Perhaps this child's manner of arrival should have prepared me for future trouble, but it took me by surprise when, a few days later, in the middle of an otherwise peaceful family movie night, Kenna suddenly stopped nursing. She went on a nursing strike for about a week. To this day I have no idea what happened or how we managed to keep her alive, because she would not take a bottle either. Mercifully, the day Ted had to leave to finish out his deployment in Florida, Kenna inexplicably began nursing again. The challenges this child brought kept me on my knees, that's for sure!

Chapter 9
Lucan Thaniel

No doubt about it, Kenna had the family wrapped around her tiny fingers despite her tendency to crawl into the dirty mop water bucket or onto the dishwasher. I knew guardian angels worked overtime with this one when I discovered her standing on top of the upstairs hallway desktop built against a half-wall overlooking a 16-foot drop to the ceramic tile below. (I didn't know she could climb onto a chair, let alone beyond that!) The Lord tested my patience and my wits with this child.

Truly, I was learning (slowly) to be more like Jesus as I mothered the children He had given me. I was a completely different person than I had been when I graduated college and set out to change the world. Instead of molding the hearts and minds of teenagers in a public school classroom, I was wiping bottoms and rescuing a toddler who found climbing furniture preferable to playing with innocuous toys. To be sure, I wore a teacher's hat as well—by this time I had taught three children to read, write, and do arithmetic, plus a host of other educational activities. It was a far cry from analyzing Shakespeare or identifying poetic devices, yet I realized I wouldn't change a thing even if given the opportunity.

My home business gave me a unique outlet and the opportunity to build relationships outside my church and homeschool circles. I attended our company convention in the summer of 2008 and was astonished to learn I had earned a spot in the top 100. It had been a successful year; I had earned the trip to Hawaii and looked forward to taking our whole family. But...as it turned out, I had to cash out the trip instead of going in person.

Why? Because our next baby was due smack in the middle of the Hawaii travel dates. Figures! I had also had to cash out the Panama Canal cruise I earned in 2007. Not only was I not allowed to bring an infant aboard (Kenna would have been under 12 weeks old), but also my husband was deployed at the time. Having babies was ruining my world travel plans!

At least we had plenty of adventure at home, right?! And learning our baby was a boy sent me scouring baby name books. I found myself drawn to the sounds of Irish and Gaelic names and finally found one I loved: Lucan, Irish for light. I liked the meaning of Nathaniel (Hebrew: gift from God) but wanted to stick with our two-syllable naming system. I discovered "Thaniel" listed in the variations of Nathaniel, so there we had it.

Lucan was due at the end of March, but my body went into contraction mode about a month early. Since Kenna had arrived two weeks prior to her due date, we found ourselves scrambling to make arrangements for child care one evening when contractions were increasing in intensity and frequency. After getting everything in order, we made the half-hour drive to the hospital only to learn that I was not, in fact, in labor. I spent the majority of the month of March wondering if I was going into labor or not. It was annoying and a bit embarrassing, since we made a second frantic trip to the hospital later in the month only to go home yet again. This was my fifth delivery! Why was this happening?!

The night of March 26 we went—again—to the hospital, and I told them I was not leaving without a baby in my arms! The doctor on duty assured me I was definitely in labor and told everyone to be on alert, because I was going to sneeze and this baby would "fall out."

Boy, was she wrong.

By the time I was admitted, I had been undergoing contractions for hours upon hours. I was exhausted upon arrival and had already given up on the idea of having another natural birth—I simply had no more tolerance for the pain which I felt I had endured all month. I got an epidural, and the doctor left, expecting to be called back soon. But nothing happened. Finally, an examination revealed that the baby was face up. Since I was numb (theoretically), the doctor tried manually turning Lucan, to no avail.

From midnight to 4 a.m. I pushed on and off with the help and encouragement of a nurse who looked so sympathetic to my plight. Ted nodded off in the chair beside me, and who could blame him? He wasn't in pain, and we had been at this for just about forever. Finally the doctor announced she was going to use the vacuum, and if that didn't work, we would have an emergency C-section. I cried out to the Lord in pure exhaustion and desperation. I remember squeezing Ted's hand and begging him to pray the baby would come out, because I just couldn't do this anymore.

Hallelujah and praise Jesus, with that little bit of extra help, our boy came out purple and squalling. His forehead bore the marks of our ineffective efforts to usher him into the world, but they faded in time, and Lucan Thaniel was otherwise a very healthy boy. My recovery was a bit more significant, but I was thankful that at least I didn't also have to recover from a C-section after laboring for over 25 hours (or was it 25 days?!).

As Kenna had done during her nursing-through-the-night phase, Lucan slept in our closet in the early months. Thankfully he was a wonderful eater—like clockwork, every three hours. Great during the day...not so much at night. He was a pretty mellow little fellow, which was a welcome quality in an already bustling household.

Lucan's arrival meant it was time to upgrade our vehicle. We paid cash for a three-year-old Suburban, having finally made the last payments on the minivan we had purchased brand new in 2003 when I was pregnant with Arden. (How did we not realize how much money we were paying in interest?! I vowed never to buy another brand new vehicle again!) We gave Ted's Saturn to a young couple in ministry. "Alex" had served us well during our 12 years of marriage, but an old two-door car needed a smaller family to cart around.

After four years in Las Vegas, it was time to hit the road for our next assignment—back to Wright-Patterson AFB in Ohio. We looked forward to reconnecting with friends and being in a familiar setting.

I spent many late nights timing contractions with Lucan and apparently feeling a bit snarky. I discovered this old blog post I had written on March 14, 2007:

You Know You're "Over" Being Pregnant When...

1. Your ankles are as big as your knees.

2. The only shoes you ever wear are flip-flops, no matter what the temperature.

3. You've outgrown your maternity clothes.

4. After struggling to take your ring off to apply lotion, you start to think it wouldn't really be that bad if people mistake you for an unwed mother.

5. Between having contractions, leg cramps, and a nearly continually full bladder, you actually believe you'll get more sleep after the baby arrives.

6. Your Bible study takes on a whole new perspective: "Deliver me, O Lord..."

7. Your toddler closes the dishwasher by standing up and using her leg to kick the door upwards...because that's the only way she remembers seeing YOU close it.

8. You seriously consider sleeping outside under the full moon to see if there's any truth to the idea of going into labor during that phase.

9. Your idea of sweeping the floor is to kick the Cheerios underneath the cabinets where they can't be immediately seen.

10. You silently dare anyone to ask you "How much longer?!"

Chapter 10
The Birth Control Decision, Part 2

In 2010 I was determined to get "back in shape." During our stint in Las Vegas I had learned to love running as a way to pursue fitness and time alone. I had good intentions after our move to Ohio, but the weather differences plus nursing a baby made it easy to justify not going at all. I gave into a current fitness craze and bought an exercise program I could do at home. Ted joined me during some of the workout days, and while I can't say I hated every minute of the long, grueling sessions, I probably hated 90% of the minutes. I was so proud when, 90 days later, I could say I had completed the program altogether! Unfortunately, my before and after pictures were not as compelling of a change as I had hoped. I began to feel frustrated with the idea that I was already "past my prime." After having our first four babies, I was able to bounce back fairly quickly—while I definitely had a "mom bod," I never really changed sizes or felt too drastically different from my pre-childbearing days. But after Lucan was born, it seemed much harder to get back into shape.

Toward the end of this 90-day exercise regimen, I found one reason, perhaps, that I was having difficulty achieving the toned physique I had envisioned: I was pregnant again. I struggled with feelings of being overwhelmed—it seemed that was my typical, fleshly response at seeing those two pink lines. I didn't understand why some women who wanted children couldn't get pregnant, and here we were with five healthy kids and another one on the way. It didn't seem fair—I hadn't asked for a large family, just as my friends hadn't asked for the pain of infertility. Why didn't God balance things out a little?

And then it started—the spotting. The bleeding. I was still only a few weeks along. I had an ultrasound that showed a heartbeat, so I took comfort from that and decided just to be careful. No need to exercise, let alone strenuously. I was glad my program was finished.

Wright-Patterson's medical center is a teaching hospital, and while I was there to check on the baby, I saw a notice asking for volunteers in the early stages of pregnancy who were willing to allow medical students to do ultrasounds. Since I have always loved seeing our babies in utero, I told the staff I would happy to help. (Plus, I figured, it would allow me the opportunity to peek on our little one to check his or her status again.)

The doctor in charge of this particular program contacted me a few days later, and we scheduled a time for me to return so he and a student could perform the ultrasound. By the time that appointment arrived, I had experienced more spotting. I kept myself somewhat emotionally detached; I was able to speak frankly with the doctor about the possibility that in the few short days since the last time I had come for an ultrasound, I may very well have lost the baby.

My intuition was correct. There was no heartbeat. Unlike the doctor who had informed me about my first miscarriage, this man was extremely kind and compassionate. I was not nearly as emotional as I had been in the emergency room in Las Vegas, which was probably good for the poor student who sat through this whole exchange. I spoke openly about my faith, that God had His plans and purposes, and we were thankful for the children He had already given us. The doctor wished me well, and I walked to the parking lot and sat in the minivan alone. It was then that I shed tears for a lost little soul whom I would never have the opportunity to know on earth. I was only seven weeks along, barely having gotten used to the idea of being pregnant. Yet already my mind had shifted, thinking ahead to the future—how the room set-ups could be made, how we would rearrange car seats and booster seats, how our school year breaks would need to be planned—so many things I had already mentally decided—suddenly irrelevant. Just like that.

I had no idea whether this little being was a boy or a girl, and honestly, I didn't have the emotional strength to go on a journey of grief similar to the one I had traveled four years earlier. I allowed myself to be sad and gave myself space, expecting some mental and emotional turmoil like I had experienced previously, but it was different. I didn't know why—but I did struggle with feeling guilty that I was not as sad as before. Had I known somehow that we would lose this pregnancy? Was I really that detached? Or was I secretly relieved, just a little bit, that God took something from me that I didn't feel I could handle anyway? I hated to even put words to that thought. But it was there. My thoughts and emotions were a tangled mess, but eventually I found solace in God's Word, my Rock when I couldn't trust myself, my feelings, or my circumstances.

I began praying very specifically about our family. My heart was broken in recognizing the pattern of ultimate selfishness with which I continued to struggle when it came to matters of taking up my cross and serving my family daily. More kids means more work, and I so rarely had time "to myself" as it was. I loved Charis, Tobin, Arden, Kenna, and Lucan so completely. Every time a new baby joined our family, I marveled at how love multiplies. We never have to worry about there not being enough love to go around! Our hearts simply expand more and more. And yet…I never felt "ready" for the next child. I never felt I "could handle" one more.

On the other hand, neither Ted nor I felt comfortable taking permanent measures to stop having children. I understood why some of our friends were making those kinds of decisions, sometimes for physical health reasons due to complicated pregnancies, sometimes for other, more private reasons—but either way, I felt no judgment toward their decisions. I simply did not feel that the Lord had given us the freedom to make that choice.

I considered these things and continued to pour out my heart to the Lord, asking Him for guidance. Really, I just wanted Him to spell out His will for our family! How many children did He want to give us?! Then I could decide if I was going to continue to be a willing participant in this plan! But of course, that isn't how God works. And I was desperately desiring for my husband and me to be in complete agreement, whatever that might look like. I hated that our charting caused us to be more focused on trying to avoid pregnancy than allowing us to experience true marital unity and intimacy the way God undoubtedly intended.

And honestly, when I looked at our charts, the times I did get pregnant—well, those were the times my body strayed from its otherwise extremely regular pattern. It was almost as if God smilingly manipulated things j-u-s-t enough in order to let me feel somewhat "in control." Meanwhile He was patiently waiting for the right time to plant in my womb the little being He had designed from before the foundations of the world.

I talked with Ted about my conflicted feelings. I presented my case to him: if we truly believed God is good and that He is sovereign, and if we were already trusting Him with our family dynamics *to an extent*, were we ready to take the next step of faith? Were we ready to abandon our seeming need to control things? Hadn't the

Lord shown us twice now that He creates and takes life according to His own divine purposes? We now had two babies in heaven whom we know God loved and created just as He had our earthly babies.

Furthermore, was it really for the good of our marriage to refrain from being intimate simply for the sake of preventing a pregnancy we didn't feel ready for? What if we decided that we truly trusted God, once and for all, and allowed ourselves to experience the full and complete joy of total abandonment?

I'm not sure Ted needed convincing after I got to that last part...but I do know that as a couple, we were not ready to make that leap of faith four years prior. Now, however, we were. Happily I quit charting—I stopped informing Ted whether or not we were "safe." We spent the next half year or so enjoying complete freedom within our marriage, and each month that passed with me not becoming pregnant seemed to confirm our decision. We probably "should" have gotten pregnant!

And then we got some news that would change our family dynamics for the foreseeable future.

Chapter 11
Zaden Ezekiel

After years of being non-deployable because of his medical code for asthma, Ted's time had come. The Air Force doctors signed a medical waiver, and we had a few months to prepare for Ted to deploy to Kandahar, Afghanistan for a full year. He left in April 2011 for a month of training, came home for a few days, and shipped out in May for the desert. When we said our final goodbyes, I was six months pregnant with our next boy. Confirmation of the pregnancy came right about the time we learned Ted would be gone not only for the birth, but also for the first 9 months of our baby's life. I wondered at God's timing—and yet we had complete peace that everything was happening exactly as God ordained it.

Over the years I have heard many folks say with a shake of their heads, "I don't know how you do it. I could never [watch my husband leave for a war zone; spend a year apart; homeschool my kids; have that many babies; whatever]."

The truth is, we do what we have to. I knew I was marrying an Air Force man. I may not have completely understood what that meant for our lifestyle, but I knew, more or less, that my husband had committed himself to serving our country, and that would sometimes mean separations. As for homeschooling, that was another call God placed on our lives years earlier, and six years in, we were hooked. None of us could envision doing school any differently. (Trust me, I had my days when I pleaded with God to let me send my kids to school, especially during that deployment year! Seeing the yellow bus stop at our corner every morning was very tempting!) And as for having more babies, well, obviously we weren't doing anything to limit our family size at this point.

So there was nothing to do but move forward. This all came about in our second year of our second assignment at Wright-Patterson AFB. We felt grateful that God had allowed us to be in a strong community, with a church family we had known since 2001 and a neighborhood that rallied around us. Though I briefly considered packing the kids up and moving home with my parents, practicality won out—we had a nice, large home with a wonderful support system and access to military medical care. My folks came to visit us multiple times and were also a big help. My mom has always made time to be with us for the birth of her grandbabies and weeks following!

Thus began one of the hardest years of our lives. We weren't quite in the smart phone age, but we did have access to Skype and Facebook, making communication much easier than in the early days of our marriage when Ted deployed to places such as Turkey, Oman, and Bahrain. The kids got to see Daddy and talk with him at least a couple of times a week if not more. I tried to make life as normal as possible, doing as much as I could to help the kids get to various events and activities. They were ages 10, 9, 7, 4, and 2 when we said our goodbyes, and The Year Daddy Was in Afghanistan will be forever etched in their minds. It had a profound influence on all of them in ways we will likely never fully understand.

I remember having a much harder time picking out this child's name than some of our other ones. For one thing, all three of our other boy names ended with the letter N. I hadn't meant for that to happen, but Tobin and Arden had a nice ring to their two names (which are often spoken as if they are one unit, TobinandArden, since the boys do so much together). After Lucan came along, it seemed we had a pattern and it wouldn't be quite right if the next boy's name didn't match it. So I narrowed my focus to names ending in N. Additionally, I had decided somewhere along the line that we would not repeat initials. This made labeling items easier as well as leaving notes or texts! So I completely skipped the names in sections C, T, A, K, and L.

With these self-imposed constraints, I finally made my way to the Z section, not expecting to find much of anything. I was both surprised and delighted to find a name I had never heard before that fit all of our criteria! Zaden is Dutch and means *sower of seeds*. While our now seven-year-old Zaden jokes that he will someday be a farmer, the prayer behind his name's meaning is that our son will sow seeds of the gospel of Christ, leading many souls to heaven.

We broke the two-syllable mold for his middle name. With the more traumatic circumstances that our family was facing at the time, Ezekiel (Hebrew: *God is my strength*) seemed an appropriate reminder. I am not a fan of the supposed doctrine that God will not give us more than we can handle. I do not find that anywhere in the pages of Scripture. In fact, I believe God often gives us more than we can handle—much more. It is during these times that HE shows Himself powerfully in our lives. It is then that He makes His name glorious, revealing His character and care-acting on our behalf. The idea that God won't give me more than I can handle seems a bit prideful, actually; I certainly would not have assumed I could handle having a sixth child while my husband worked in a war zone!

Ted would receive two weeks of "R and R" during his year away from us, and we chose for him to come home about two-thirds of the way through the deployment. This meant, of course, that he would miss Zaden's birth, but we figured it would be easier mentally to say goodbye again knowing we had "only" four months of separation left. So when we made the trip to the hospital early in the morning on August 24, 2011, we were hoping to connect with Ted via the Daddy Cam at the hospital, a video camera that supposedly would allow Ted to view the birth from the base in Kandahar. Unfortunately, the timing was off, since the person running the system did not arrive until after the big event had already happened. But they were able to connect the phone lines, so we communicated the old-fashioned way: on a telephone with a curly cord. I suppose it was better than nothing, but I imagine it left a lot to be desired!

Meanwhile, my mom and Charis were attending the birth with me while a neighbor stayed at the house with the other children. Our midwife was so wonderful—she was delighted Charis had come along to observe and help. This was a decision I had talked over with Ted before he deployed, and then I asked Charis if she would like to be present when her baby brother was born. Did she ever! She was so excited! We watched a birthing documentary beforehand and talked through everything. She was remarkable, staying so calm and offering encouragement to me throughout the labor process. The look on her face when the midwife told her to don some gloves so she could catch Zaden! Eagerly she followed directions, and before we knew it, my firstborn child, ten-year-old Charis, was holding our sixth baby...before his mother got to snuggle him!

On the other side of the world, Ted heard the cries of his newborn son and received assurances that all was well with both Mom and baby. From Ted's perspective, something else that made the day extra special came from the fact that it was Ramadan in Afghanistan, and the advisors were hosting their Afghan counterparts for an Iftar dinner that night[3]. In addition to the scheduled party, Ted had the honor of announcing his son had been born that day. In their culture, this is a big deal, so they ended up all celebrating Zaden as they feasted. Ted got lots of hearty, back-slapping hugs and scratchy-beard kisses on both cheeks. According to Ted, none of them could pronounce Zaden's name, but their excitement was contagious anyway!

You would think nursing five children previously would mean I was at least a competent breastfeeding mother if not a complete pro by this time. But I was stunned to learn at Zaden's two-week check-up that he had lost a whole pound off his birth weight (which had been a decent 8 pounds, 3 ounces). The doctor instructed me to supplement with formula, a complete and utter devastation. I cried in the lactation consultant's office, then wiped my tears and worked with her to formulate a plan. The next month was possibly one of the most stressful periods of my entire life up until then. I was determined to nurse my baby, and I utilized a hospital-grade pump and a supplemental nursing system along with more time, effort, sweat, and tears than I'm sure anyone wants to read about. The moment Zaden's doctor approved his weight gain and told me to "keep doing what you're doing" was a huge victory for me—because by this point I had ditched the formula and had no intentions of going back. After nearly a month, I also

[3] This is the celebratory breaking of the fast after the sun goes down.

76

ditched the supplemental nursing system and the hospital pump. Zaden was able to nurse completely on his own. Such a gift! And such a triumph! But I will say I learned a completely different perspective on the whole breastfeeding issue, and I completely understand why so many moms quit nursing. Mamas, feed your babies however you can feed them!

During these early days of Zaden's life, I chose to do an online Bible study at home instead of packing everyone up to attend our weekly women's study at church—much less stress and a lot more study happened. One morning while the house was still quiet, I listened to Priscilla Shirer teaching on the book of Jonah (subtitle: *A Life Interrupted*, and you can bet this study was written especially for me!). The lesson included a word study on the Greek word *rhema*[4], "specific word from the Lord." As Priscilla talked about how Jonah had received a "rhema word" from God telling Him to go preach to Ninevah, I received my own "rhema word" from the Lord. I didn't hear an audible voice, but I did clearly understand the Lord speaking to my spirit. He told me, "There will be a girl, and you will name her Rhema." I gasped out loud, put my pen down, and paused the video. My heart was beating inside my chest, and I actually looked around because the words were that real to me. And then I laughed. Like Abraham's wife Sarah, I laughed. *Really, God? I'm nursing my baby boy right now, and you're telling me we'll have a girl? When?*

---

[4] We pronounce it RAY-muh.

But God was silent on that one! I journaled about my thoughts, prayed on it, and tucked it away in my heart for later. For now, it was enough—more than enough—to hold and care for my baby boy, loving him along with his older brothers and sisters, while his daddy worked on the other side of the world.

Chapter 12
Seanin Gabriel

T ed told the kids that every day in Afghanistan would buy us three days in Europe as a family, and the Air Force obliged and sent us to Naples, Italy, upon completion of his deployment. We had time for a 30-day road trip (we called it the "Jacobson Farewell Tour,") and just before Zaden turned one year old, we boarded a plane to cross the ocean.

We reveled in this change—everywhere we went we could see Mt. Vesuvio. Gelato, coffee, and cornetti became favorites. And for a homeschooling family, access to ancient Greek and Roman ruins was educational as well as fun! We embraced every opportunity to learn about our culture and the history surrounding us. Language studies were slower than we may have liked, but we persevered. After what seemed an eternity squished into a two-bedroom apartment on base, we moved into a beautiful, spacious rental in town with three floors of tiled, echo-chamber living space.

We spent my birthday (Thanksgiving 2012) exploring the island of Capri, bringing one of the kids' school read-alouds to life (although we had to wait to see the Blue Grotto during a later visit). It was off season on the island, which was perfect for us—hardly any other tourists. The weather cooperated beautifully, and though our hike was longer and more strenuous than we maybe anticipated, the kids were troopers. I told them my best birthday present was that they did not complain the whole day! As we passed doorways of houses and shops on the narrow, winding roads, people would pop outside to stare at us. We could hear them counting quietly, "Uno, due, tre, quattro, cinque, sei...sei?! Sei bambini? Ay! Mamma mia!" It gave us quite the chuckle. To be sure, our family was a novelty in the Italian culture. Most families had one or two children at the most, and everyone piled into tiny little roller skate cars. Our big white Suburban with all its passengers drew stares wherever we went, and even on the highway we could see fingers pointing and knew riders were trying to get a head count before they passed us.

So when we learned another baby would join us in 2013, we had some fun with our pregnancy announce-ment video.[5] Sette bambini?! Ay! Mamma mia! Zaden would be almost exactly two years old when Baby #7

---

joined us. I just knew it would be a girl, and at least we already had her first name picked out.

The pregnancy progressed well, and life continued with adventures big and small. We learned that living in Italy is an entirely different thing from touring Italy, and sometimes the drawbacks threatened to overshadow the beauty. But on the whole, we were loving our life in Napoli. Ted's job at NATO allowed him to work with people from many different countries, a privilege he held in high regard. He made it a point to learn how to say "Good morning" in every one of the 21 languages represented there at the time, a gesture that was not lost on those for whom English was a third, fourth, or fifth language. The Italian coffee culture made for strong working relationships. Much work was done at the coffee bar, and the banter between folks from different countries made for fun stories around the dinner table.

The kids and I were likewise enjoying our new normal. We loved the space and time to do our homeschool activities in our Italian villa, but we also looked forward to going to base a couple of times a week. We would gather with other homeschoolers or attend my women's Bible study, a lifeline of close connections that made living overseas especially sweet. I scheduled appointments and did our base shopping whenever we went to the Support Site to minimize the 17-mile commute.

One appointment we looked forward to especially was our ultrasound. I had no concerns by this point, having passed the first trimester long ago, but it was always reassuring to see our little one and learn that everything was all right. The tech was more than competent, with years of experience, but I couldn't help asking her, "Are you sure?!" when she told us the baby was a boy. I had been certain this baby was our girl Rhema. But clearly, the anatomy showed, we had another boy on the way.

I was stunned. Another boy? But...God had told me we would have a girl! And then I realized He hadn't said *when* that girl would come. I rolled my eyes at Him and grumbled in my spirit more than a little bit. *Not funny, God!* I am fairly certain I heard Him chuckle.

Now we had to come up with a boy name. The base library wasn't exactly a wealth of resources, but not to worry. We had plenty of time.

One hot day I spent quite a bit of time outside, and despite my efforts, I felt dehydrated. I rested at home after feeling a number of Braxton-Hicks contractions, but even after a nap and loads more water, the contractions weren't stopping. By the time evening rolled around, they were coming every few minutes. I was only 33 weeks along, and since I had experienced some similar things with other babies, I wasn't terribly concerned. Nevertheless, my friends whom I told about it *were*, so after a call to the nurses' line, my friend Carla came to pick me up and drive me to the Navy base hospital while Ted stayed home with the kids.

I kissed my husband goodbye, certain that all of this was a huge fuss over nothing. I remembered the multiple false labors with Lucan. Even with Zaden I hadn't been quite sure whether I was in real labor or not during the week or so leading up to his birth. My body just seemed to like practicing, I guess!

The ER was quiet. We were taken back and the whole rigmarole began, all the questions about this pregnancy and previous deliveries. Was I drinking water? When did the contractions start? How far apart were they? I was sent to the bathroom with a cup and then put on a monitor. Contractions continued, but none of them were painful. Carla and I talked and joked together. I just knew that I'd be sent home with instructions to put my feet up, rest, and drink lots of water. In fact, I was wishing I was home in bed doing just that!

And then the doctor came in with the lab results. We were in pre-term labor, and because the naval hospital was not set up with a NICU, I needed to go to the nearest Italian hospital. My stomach dropped. All of a sudden what had seemed like a joke was now all too incredibly real. My head swirled while everyone around me sprang into action. Words like *ambulance, steroids,* and *liaison* hovered in the air, sending waves of fear through my body and causing uncontrollable trembling.

Carla shifted into practical caregiver mode, asking all kinds of wonderful questions—will she need sheets and towels? (You do in many Italian hospitals.) What if she delivers—what happens next? What if she *doesn't* deliver? Then what? I was so thankful someone who could think clearly was there to advocate on my behalf. Some years later the tables would turn and I would find myself in the role of advocator, speaking up for a precious, vulnerable person in my life. But in that moment, I was thankful for Carla's quick thinking.

The ambulance ride felt both surreal and terrifying, but Gina, the liaison, and the Navy techs who rode with me were as kind and reassuring as could be.

We arrived at Clinica Pineta Grande, where Ted met us for another blur of activity. More examinations. Another ultrasound. Drawn blood. Paperwork. Translations. Questions. And then they took me to a private hospital room (I learned later that I probably got the royal treatment because of being an American there on military orders). More tests (using contraptions that looked suspiciously like medieval torture devices). Medicine in an IV. And then everyone who spoke English aside from my husband had gone home for the night, and we were left in peace to try to get some sleep in a hospital bed and rollaway couch that weren't any more comfortable than the ones in the USA.

I spent five days in that hospital. It was an interesting cultural experience! The food brought to me on trays at mealtimes was amazing. At times I felt like I was on vacation. Between the mouth-watering food and the opportunity to rest and read at will, I wasn't sure what to do with myself. But the uncertainty of the whole situation kept me in prayer, worship, and reading God's Word. There were too many "what ifs" for me to handle on my own. With some extra time on my hands, I got serious about finding a name for this boy—"Septimus" (Latin for *seven*) was a fun nickname but certainly not what we would call our son for his whole life. I had no access to books, so I scoured the internet and found an Irish version of the name John (my father and brother's first name). Seanin[6] means "God's gracious gift." I chose Gabriel (Hebrew: mighty man of God) for the middle name. Both my first and middle name options were on extremely short lists. Ted gave his approval to Seanin Gabriel when we had time to discuss the issue together; we figured if this baby was going to make an early appearance, we'd better have a name ready!

However, only five long-short days after the whirlwind admittance, the Italian medical team released me to go home on bedrest. Our church and homeschool communities poured out love on us over the following weeks, just as we had experienced during Ted's deployment. The Body of Christ is a precious, beautiful thing! God definitely created us for community. Life is so much better when we have a tribe with whom to experience the joys and sorrows of our journey. During this part of our journey, people brought us meals, played with and transported our kids, and wouldn't let me even think of getting out of bed. By God's grace, we made it to 37 weeks, and then I was allowed to return to a somewhat normal life.

The next two weeks were the hottest part of summer in southern Italy. We spent our evenings in the downstairs family room (one of the few rooms with a tiny bit of air conditioning) with Ted reading *The Fellowship*

---

[6] Pronounced SHANE-in.

of the Ring out loud while I timed my daily contractions. After all the hullaballoo at 33 weeks, our boy seemed content to stay right where he was despite my body's seeming concerted efforts to gear up for labor.

Finally, a week before our due date, Seanin was ready to leave his cozy womb. Though my doctor was certain I would deliver on the side of the autostrada, we made it to the hospital in plenty of time for a 4:30 a.m. delivery of our nine-pound boy on August 14, 2013. Charis and Ted were both there to welcome our healthy baby boy into the world.

God is gracious, indeed!

Chapter 13
Rhema Riyel

The dawn of 2014 had me once again ready and determined to give myself some self-care in the form of regular exercise. This year would see my fortieth birthday (November 22), and I was ready to focus on a goal I had set for myself some eight or nine years earlier: run a full marathon before I turned 40. Was I crazy? Probably. Did I have a clue what I was in for? Not at all. But I had a dream of crossing the finish line in Athens, Greece (because where else would you do a full marathon while living in Europe if not the original course?!). My dream was not simply to run the race. No, if I was going to torture myself with running 26.2 miles, I wanted it to count for something significant.

A team of about a dozen ladies joined me when I set out this vision: we would commit to training and running the marathon as a fundraiser for a local organization that had become dear to our hearts. Mission of Light/Missione di Luce, a church ministry founded about the time our family moved to Italy, reached the "untouchables" of the sprawling city of Napoli. Prostitution is, unfortunately, legal in this country, situated perfectly at the crossroads of the Mediterranean. The evils of human trafficking are on blatant display along many highways and pothole-filled back roads. My heart broke for these young women and men. When I met Joyce, co-founder of Mission of Light (soon to become my dear friend and mentor), I knew I wanted to join her in this outreach.

The ministry was young, and as of yet, there was no building, no facility, no refuge in which to receive those who chose to leave the streets. My heart longed to see a safe house become a reality, a place for Missione di Luce to be the hands and feet of Jesus, a place for rescue workers and counselors to minister to a person's body, soul, and spirit with the gospel of Christ. My marathon teammates and I chose to focus our fundraising efforts on this glaring need.

With the arrival of summer training began in earnest. I had started the year with a couch-to-5K program and was working my way up to a 10K and beyond. In July I had a foot injury that took some weeks to overcome. These weeks involved gentle stretching, self-care, a visit to the doctor, and advice from my physical therapist friend who was our team leader, having run 17 marathons herself. Finally I was back in training. Another friend who had no desire to run but

loved the idea of a girls' trip coordinated our accom-
modations and tour options for our weekend in Athens.
Moms made child care arrangements and friends from
afar booked plane tickets to join us in Greece.

By late September I seemed to be back on track
with training. Then one day I squatted down (properly
even!) to lift Seanin and something seemed to explode in
my lower back. Pain radiated down my legs and I couldn't
move. Thank the Lord the children were so responsive.
Charis took Seanin from me and the boys helped me
stand. The rest of the day passed in a blur of pain. That
was October 2. The race was five weeks away. I spent the
next few weeks recovering. I met with an Italian
physical/massage therapist several times; I visited the
chiropractor; I talked with a doctor and got some muscle
relaxants. I walked on our treadmill. And walked. And
walked. One of my workouts was 2 hours long and gave
me hope that I would, in fact, be able to finish the
marathon, even if I weren't running. I was bound and
determined I would finish that course even if I had to
crawl the last few miles.

The last weekend in October I hit the treadmill
and carefully tried some slow running. Four days in a row
I ran! Slowly, to be sure, but I ran. And I had hope.
November 9, 2014, I was going to finish a marathon!

I awoke at 3 a.m. the morning of the race, too full
of nervous energy to sleep. I used a permanent marker to
write the names of women whom Missione di Luce had
ministered to in recent weeks all up and down my left
arm. Tirzah, my running partner, and I prayed for those

women and all who are held captive as we made our way along the course later that morning. Singing praise songs and speaking prayers and Scripture as we kept our run-4-minutes-walk-1-minute intervals, we found the first 17 or 18 miles of the course went by much faster than anticipated!

I urged Tirzah (who had, after all, completed her training) to leave me behind after we reached the top of the seven-mile hill, and we continued toward the finish line at our own pace. Every single one of our teammates finished the course! I was so proud of everyone as individuals, and incredibly proud of us as a team—together we raised over $9,000 for a future Missione di Luce safe house.

The once-in-a-lifetime experience defied words (although I attempted[7]). I could hardly move after finishing the race, but within 48 hours I was making plans to do the Rome marathon four months later. My body said otherwise when, one week after the race, I realized I had taken a microscopic stowaway along with me on the course from Marathon to the Olympic Stadium. "Athena" was due in July 2015, so at least we were keeping with our pattern of having a baby approximately every two years!

We kept the secret for a few more weeks, sharing the news with our kids and my mother-in-law on our Christmas cruise, a last big family vacation before we had to pack up for America. Since our crew of seven kids

---

[7] http://proverbs4.blogspot.com/2015/02/athens-marathon-2014.html

plus Mom, Dad, and Grandma attracted attention everywhere we went, both on the ship as well as every port we toured, we had some more fun with a video announcement[8] addressing many of the comments we receive when we are out in public with such a "huge" family!

Because of the pre-term labor scare with Seanin, our doctor wanted us safely Stateside well before my due date with Rhema—for Rhema she was, the girl I had known we would have someday. Moving to rural Iowa/Nebraska from Napoli, Italia, was an unexpected culture shock, by far the most difficult PCS (permanent change of station) our family had experienced. But we were grateful for a beautiful Victorian house we could rent in the small town of Glenwood, Iowa, a short commute from Ted's duty assignment at Offutt AFB in Omaha, Nebraska. Having long ago crossed the threshold of crazy, we took it a step further by purchasing a big white van that would more easily seat our long-legged teenagers as well as the little ones.

We found another wonderful church family who embraced us and took the time to learn every child's name before we left to go home after our first Sunday morning visit. The ladies threw a baby shower for me just a few weeks after meeting me, and we felt loved and more or less settled into our new home by the time our baby girl decided to join us in the outside world.

---

[8] https://www.youtube.com/watch?v=4nNjqu9DXtQ

Around lunchtime on July 15, 2015, several intense contractions sent us grabbing our bags and rushing out the door. (The way Ted tells it, I went from complaining about being a bit uncomfortable to "Get me to the hospital NOW" within 15 minutes.) Grandma J stayed at the house with the younger kids, freeing Charis to attend the delivery of her baby sister. We sped toward the hospital, going fast enough that Ted had a plan to ask for an escort to the hospital when (not if!) we got pulled over by one of Omaha's finest—but obviously not in our big white van! (This we left at home in case Grandma needed to transport kids somewhere.) No, our record-breaking run to the hospital happened in a Dodge Charger we were borrowing because our Suburban was stuck on a cargo ship that had caught fire off the coast of England. Our truck was fine, but the incident delayed its arrival in the States by nearly three months. The loan of the speedy car that transported us to Bellevue Medical Center was just one example of God's gracious provision before we even knew we needed it.

Had Rhema not been face up, we may have had a baby in the hospital parking lot, but as it turned out, there was enough time to get situated in the birthing room. Less than an hour of effort and she emerged, face up, all perfect and beautiful, our little Rhema Riyel[9]. We chose her middle name, which is a derivation from the Hebrew *Ariel,* meaning "lioness of God," after meeting Christine Duncan. Christine is a lovely, talented singer

---

[9] We pronounce it Rye-YELL.

and songwriter who was a member of the church we attended during our two stints in Ohio. Her song lyrics are richly theological and point to an intimate, personal God worthy of our praise and honor. With her permission, we chose to use Christine's stage name *Riyel* as Rhema's middle name.

Already the Lord had given me several "rhema words," specific words from Him, regarding this sweet baby. First and foremost, of course, was the foreknowledge that this daughter would be born someday and we were to name her Rhema. I prayed other specific things concerning the circumstances surrounding Rhema's birth, and God graciously granted those requests. And finally, in the delivery room after I lay exhausted, having given birth without medication to my eighth baby who happened to arrive face up, I cried out to the Lord, "I can't do this again. Please, I can't do this again." And I felt Him assure me this would be my last such delivery. I sighed in relief at hearing this particular rhema word. This mama was tired. Delivering a baby at 40 years old is no joke. I may be able to run a marathon (slowly!), but pregnancy in one's "advanced maternal age" isn't for the fainthearted! I was blessed to have pregnancies that were relatively free of complications and severe physical difficulties, but I could tell the last few babies I carried had definitely taken a toll on my body. So I resolved to enjoy every single moment with this baby, even the middle-of-the-night feedings, since obviously she was going to be our last.

Chapter 14
The Birth Control Decision, Part 3

God told me to enjoy nursing baby Rhema, even though she woke every night for over a year demanding to be fed. (Our first few babies spoiled us, apparently, since they all began sleeping through the night between six and twelve weeks of age!) *She's your last one, and this stage will go by faster than you can imagine.* And so I tried. Late at night as I sleepily fed my baby, I tried to be intentional about giving thanks to the Lord for this privilege. I remembered the struggles with nursing her in the beginning. Like Zaden, Rhema did not gain weight as expected, although she did not lose any either—her two-week check-up had her at exactly her birth weight. I unearthed the supplemental nursing system, and we started the whole process of pumping, feeding, washing pump parts, and doing it all over again, day after day after day. I cried out of sheer exhaustion. I thought we would have avoided this with our proactive efforts in the hospital.

See, when Seanin was born, chunky boy that he was, he had no weight loss issues. But we did have nursing issues, and I was in such pain I was ready to call it quits before a couple of weeks had passed. A friend sent me information about lip ties. I had heard of tongue ties, which the lactation consultant had ruled out, but not lip ties. The more I researched, the more convinced I was that this was our problem. Out of curiosity, I made all my kids show me their mouths, and sure enough! Zaden and Kenna, the two kiddos with whom I had struggled the most to feed, each had a very pronounced upper lip frenulum! We had Seanin's released when he was four weeks old, and the improvement in nursing was immediate. So when Rhema was born, I immediately checked her mouth. Before we left the hospital her lip tie was also released.

Nevertheless, we had our issues. It took a couple of months before her weight stabilized and I felt we really had the hang of the feeding thing. It was always humbling, after having all these babies, to have struggles like these. It just goes to show that every baby is different, every mama is different, and every baby-mama relationship is different. I've learned never to make assumptions about other babies and other mamas!

Another first for me was the unexpected onslaught of post-partum depression. Oh, sure, I had been a hormonal wreck in the days and weeks following other births, but something was different this time around. I was really struggling. I was on the verge of asking my doctor about medication—and I'm the mom who declined antibiotics even though I tested positive for Group Strep-B prior to birthing babies #7 and #8. A friend reminded me of the Young Living starter kit I had purchased when we were in Italy. I had ordered it to boost our family's immune system (I was sick and tired of being sick and tired and having the kids fall like dominoes every time one person brought home a sniffle). Yet I found significant emotional and mental support in those tiny little bottles. The week after Mother's Day 2016 I was such a wreck my husband was doing research on antidepressants and asking for other people's advice. But by the grace of God, I remembered the support I had received months before by using Frankincense and Joy (an essential oil blend). What could have been a devastating time for me and my family ended as suddenly as it had begun—and though I could not know it at the time, the experience helped prepare me for the most difficult part of our journey yet.

We were headed into summer 2016 feeling optimistic. Rhema was getting closer to sleeping through the night more consistently, and I was so happy and content with our family size. What a beautiful ending for our family planning story, I thought, a journey that taught us to trust God for our family size. I could trace His hand so clearly every step of the way. Though we began our marriage trying to control every aspect of our lives, God showed us how much more beautiful His plan was. Watching it unfold had brought both joy and peace—not to mention little people I couldn't imagine not having in our lives. And here we were, on the other side of having babies. God had told me, hadn't He, that we were finished? To enjoy Rhema because she was the last one? I trusted Him completely. He had told me she would come to us years before she was conceived, and now here she was. I felt so happy and grateful for each of my eight children. Yet I was also happy and grateful to now be moving on to the next phase of our lives. The thought of taking permanent measures to ensure our family stayed the same size did not even enter my mind, because I had God's plan all figured out. He would simply close my womb, because we had birthed all the babies He planned to send us. What a beautiful, precious story of faith and family!

Mmmm hmmm.

But the story wasn't finished. And I was entirely unprepared for the next chapter to unfold. When I learned I was pregnant—AGAIN—in June 2016, I was not only overwhelmed, I was angry. I felt God had betrayed me. I was so sure He had told me I wouldn't have another baby, and here we were. Did that mean we would lose this child? Or that I had heard Him wrong? Or was He toying with my heart? I didn't like any of those options. The God I had come to know and love and trust wasn't like that. But I fought with Him anyway. If I couldn't hear from Him in a way that gave me confidence, how could I follow Him in everyday matters? How could I distinguish His voice from my own desires? For, yes, it was my desire that Rhema be our last baby. For years I had kept my heart open to God's will, trusting Him with my body, my marriage, our family. But I was tired. I had a one-year-old, two teenagers, and five children in between. It took all my time and energy to do what I did every day for my family—and I felt as if I didn't even do that very well. (I am fairly certain that a universal struggle of mothers is dealing with the constant barrage of internal messages telling us we aren't doing "enough.") And while I felt stretched in so many directions, countless women had aching hearts and empty arms. Why was I given the calling to bear so many children when so many others prayed for even one child?

I wrestled with feelings I couldn't even identify. I felt tremendous disappointment with God, but I also hated the weakness of faith I saw within myself. After years of trusting God with our family size—a counter-cultural decision based on prayer, study of Scripture, and the leading we felt for our own lives—it was all over. My faith, apparently, was not big enough; I could not fully trust God in this area after all. Not that He wasn't worthy of my trust—I knew deep down that He was! But I was too weak. God had changed my heart and my life by shaping my perspective over the years, but I couldn't keep going like this indefinitely.

How I wanted the story to be different! How I wanted to glorify the Lord with the testimony of our family! I wanted to be able to tell people He is trustworthy in all areas, including our family size. I felt that being pregnant again—and sincerely desiring to stop having babies—I was ready to move forward with taking some permanent measures. And I somehow felt as if going in that direction meant I would lose a part of the faith that had grown and shaped me. I knew I wouldn't live with regret over what "might have been" concerning babies being born, but rather that I got to a point where I simply could not find the faith to continue this journey to which God had specifically called us as a couple. Sadness filled my heart. I had thought we would have an incredible story: "We trusted God with our family planning and it all turned out beautifully!"

Instead, it looked as if our story would be: "We trusted God with our family size, got overwhelmed when it just wasn't stopping, and took matters into our own hands." Not exactly the testimony I thought we'd be sharing.

God gently reminded me during one of my Bible reading times that I am not the defender of His glory. He alone is the Great I Am. He wills and works His own good purposes. He knew my heart, and He knew our desires to honor Him. I cried; I wrote in my prayer journal; and I threw myself into my summer Bible study, *The Armor of God*[10] by Priscilla Shirer (author of the Jonah study I had done five years previously). The title of Day 1 was "Wrestling Match," and indeed I felt as if I were Jacob wrestling with the Lord through the darkness of night.

We spent a week digging into the "belt of truth" in this study. One of the questions in my workbook was this: "What are some things in your life—even good things—

---

[10] Based on Ephesians 6:10-18.

that need to be tucked away for now to keep you moving forward to the next level with God?" I struggled to answer this question and pondered it for several days before having an "aha" moment. I wondered if my fertility was part of my answer—that the blessing of a fertile womb is a good thing, yes. But after having all these children, was the "am I pregnant or not" uncertainty going to hinder me from moving forward with God?

I continued writing in my prayer journal. The Apostle Paul was prevented many times from going places he desired to go. Later God opened those doors. It wasn't a matter of right versus wrong but rather a matter of timing. Going to a particular place was wrong at this time but right at that time.

Furthermore (I wrote in my journal), though I've said many times our family and faith journey is *ours* and I would never presume to prescribe it for others...I wondered if subconsciously there was a spiritual pride issue at stake. I wondered if our decision to "let God control our family size" was something feeding my spiritual ego. Perhaps God was leading me through a change in my convictions to help prevent this from happening. I was earnestly seeking truth in the muddle of my emotions and circumstances. All truth is God's truth. And truth is...TRUE...for all people in all places at all times. So if God allows some people the peace and even direction in using human intervention for birth control (means other than those that are abortifacients), then this issue is not a truth issue (right versus wrong) but rather a timing issue. If we are seeking God's heart in this matter, asking Him for wisdom, desiring to honor Him, then—if we prayerfully moved forward with a specific decision concerning family planning, could we assume we would be making that decision within God's will? I felt the answer was yes. Something that we had not felt the freedom to do in the past wasn't necessarily off limits in the present, as long as it didn't violate Scriptural commands that stand regardless of time period or circumstances.

I began praying God would unite my husband and me once again as He had so faithfully done over our years of marriage. I prayed He would make us one in spirit and purpose, that as a couple we would be like-minded and seek the Lord's heart over our own desires. I prayed we would not make decisions from our human emotions but rather from a quiet confidence that the Lord God was indeed directing our lives.

About a month later, over the Fourth of July weekend, I woke with horrible back pain and cramping on the right side of my body. I had never experienced that kind of pain before, and when I wasn't feeling better even after staying home from church to rest, Ted and I decided it warranted a trip to the ER. I was concerned about a possible tubal pregnancy. After five hours, the doctor couldn't say why I was having pain, but an ultrasound confirmed the baby was in the right place with a strong heartbeat. I didn't think it was coincidence that the focus of our Bible study that week was *peace*. The scare of what might be happening with my body and with our baby had brought forth different emotions—I wanted this child!

Somewhere over the course of a few short weeks I had gone from anger to acceptance and even a tiny little bit of eagerness. I still felt overwhelmed and inadequate, but I knew God's grace is always sufficient; His power is always made perfect in our weaknesses. And boy, was I weak! So weak that one short month after this experience I was journaling and working through more rebellious feelings about having another baby. Fickle emotions!

Meanwhile, Ted and I had come to the decision that baby #9 would be our last. After much prayer, we felt peace about taking permanent measures. We believe God has definite purposes for each of the children He had given us as well as for our family as a whole, and we also believed our prayer-covered decision honored Him just as much as our earlier decision to let Him choose when to send us another baby.

I will forever be grateful the Lord led us to this conclusion when He did. It was a decision made out of love and prayer. Had we waited any longer, the choice would have been fear-driven, for we were about to embark on a road none of us would have chosen.

Chapter 15
Verity Irene

The phone call came just after breakfast and prayer time with the kids. I stepped into a different room so I could hear the voice on the other end. I had expected a conversation about scheduling our 20-week ultrasound. Instead, I heard phrases that sounded like a foreign language to me: *Trisomy 18* and *Edwards syndrome*. I struggled to understand what the doctor was telling me. My blood tests had shown an elevated risk for this genetic disorder resulting from cells having an extra eighteenth chromosome. Though the doctor assured me my risk was only 1 out of 10 (compared to 1 out of 187 based on my oh-so-advanced-maternal age), I couldn't get the leaden feeling out of my stomach. The doctor told me they would schedule a diagnostic ultrasound at the University of Nebraska Medical Center as soon as possible. Before we hung up, I had to ask—what was the prognosis if the baby *did* have this condition? The answer was clinical. Likely the baby would be stillborn, but if not, it would be a brief, difficult life with severe complications.

I returned to the kitchen where my children were waiting for me. There was no hiding this information. I remember telling my kids, with tears streaming down my face, "We still have a 90% chance that our baby is just fine. But no matter what happens, we know that God is good, and God is sovereign, and we are going to praise Him no matter what."

I dismissed the kids to go do something—anything. I called Ted at work and sobbed my way through the news. He prayed with me over the phone, and I hung up and cried all over again. I contacted two of my dearest friends and prayer partners. And then I put Rhema in the stroller, asked the teens to babysit the other kids, and walked to our pastor's house a few blocks away. We sat in the driveway as I poured out our news to him. Pastor Jon is a very compassionate man anyway, but his and his wife's experience of losing their firstborn halfway through the pregnancy made him especially tender-hearted toward our situation. I appreciated his prayers on behalf of our family.

က၆၈၁၆၈၃က၆၈၁၆၈၃က

The next morning I wrote the following in my prayer journal:

"My soul finds rest in God alone—my salvation comes from Him. He alone is my rock and my salvation;

He is my fortress, I will never be shaken." (Psalm 62:1-2, NIV) Oh, God! Whatever we learn Monday at the ultrasound—it won't change who you are! It won't change my passion for you; at least it won't make me turn away from you. I trust you fully because you are worthy of my trust. I desire to give you glory no matter what. You know my heart—it's yours.

You also know my weaknesses and frailties. You know my fears. My anxieties. My needs. Your grace is sufficient. Hold me close, Lord. These next three days will seem so long. And then...what? "Each day has enough trouble of its own." Let me be a seeker of your kingdom.

We—Charis, Ted, and myself—met with a genetic counselor for an hour-long consultation immediately prior to the ultrasound. She was kind, compassionate, and knowledgeable, teaching us in easy-to-understand terms what my blood test results had shown and what the doctor would be looking for in the upcoming ultrasound. I had (probably unwisely) done a bit of my own research over the weekend, and the analysis was grim. Mortality rates for babies with Edwards syndrome were extremely high, both prior to and after birth.

After 96 hours of waiting, it was time—a time we had all anticipated and dreaded. I was ready and yet so unprepared. I felt rather nauseated and yet somehow perfectly calm.

Our ultrasound tech was young and energetic, but we could tell she was careful in selecting her words. We didn't expect to hear much in the way of diagnostics, but we were eager to learn the gender of our baby, the one normal aspect of this whole process. We love getting to meet our babies in utero! What a beautiful thing it is to see a tiny person wiggling around inside my belly, even as I can feel little movements.

The first thing we saw was "the string of pearls," a beautiful spine. Baby was face down at first, but that position didn't last long. Eventually we learned that our active little wiggle-monster was a girl.

Ted and I have seen enough ultrasounds to know that our baby was different in at least one respect. I waited—longed to see—those little hands opening and closing. I had never wanted to see that "Hi, Mom!" pose so badly, a snapshot we have in other baby books lining our shelves, a beautiful profile with a little hand waving. But our baby never waved. Her hands remained in clenched fists, one of the common problems associated with Trisomy 18.

Aside from the flailing fists, we really were not sure what to make of the whole ordeal. It seemed to take so long to get all the required measurements and photos. The tech even returned to the room after leaving so that she could attempt to get some better takes—we noticed that she zoned in on the top of the baby's head and her heart.

After what seemed an eternity, a doctor entered the room to speak with us. (I was so incredibly grateful to learn that they would not send us away from the medical center without some answers: how difficult it would have been to have to go home and wait some more!) The doctor noted several concerning things from the ultrasound, all of which are characteristic of Trisomy 18:

- clenched fists, as we had already observed
- clubbed feet
- small head (measuring in the fifth percentile)
- fluid on the brain.

While she said the ultrasound results did not show specific problems with the heart, she verbally indicated that there were some suspicious aspects that made them wonder; however, the official report did not mention anything concerning the baby's heart. Based on these findings, we followed through with an amniocentesis, the first I have ever experienced in all my pregnancies.

The very few people who knew of our situation at that point were praying, and it was evident. Even as I tried to hold back tears, I listened to the soundtrack in my head playing the words, "It is well with my soul."

We were told that the initial results of the amnio would come as soon as the next day, with the final analysis finished within a week or so. Numbly I received more papers—Ted held quite the growing stack by this point. We scheduled another ultrasound for October 24, and finally the ordeal was over. We had spent nearly four hours in the university medical center. But the hardest part was to come: sharing with our parents and our other children what we had learned and then waiting—for what? Confirmation that our baby girl really did have

Edwards syndrome? We knew. We knew! The DNA analysis hadn't even begun, but in our hearts we were already on that road.

CRITICAL ORNAMENT

Later that night, after we put the younger children to bed, we sat down with the older four kids and outlined the information we had received. It was a peaceful, calm conversation. Some tears were shed, but the Holy Spirit was tangibly present. We allowed the kids to ask or say anything they wanted, and though a few questions surfaced, for the most part they were very, very quiet. Our nine-year-old daughter was the most visibly distraught—thankfully she was sitting by her daddy and snuggled up close.

We shared our baby's name with the children during that time together, and the next day we shared with our prayer circles. We wanted people to be praying for our little girl by name, and we wanted anyone who followed our journey to think of her as a person in utero. While the Name of the Baby had always been a Well-Kept Secret in our family, this situation was obviously much different. We did not know how long we would have this little girl on earth. One of the stirrings of our hearts was to proclaim the truth about Life—it is a gift from God, the Creator, and He makes no mistakes. The morning's Bible reading for me that day included Psalm 116, and one verse states, "Precious in the sight of the Lord is the death of his saints" (v. 15). We know from

108

Psalm 139 that our lives are precious in His sight as well, and while I don't deny that I had a good, ugly cry for awhile as I read my Bible, I am so incredibly grateful at the way God's Word is living and active and speaks to us.

And so, we introduced our loved ones and extended circles of friends to our baby girl, Verity Irene.

Verity...Truth.

Irene...Peace.

The name Verity was on my heart from the very beginning of this pregnancy—God plainly spoke His Truth to me not only about our very specific situation (long before we had even heard about Trisomy 18), but He also continued to press His eternal truths on our hearts. We prayed then, as we still pray, that we can share those truths with others along this journey.

Irene, my mother's first name and my middle name, is Greek for "peace." And it was so, so obvious that God was pouring out His peace that passes all understanding all during the weekend as we waited on pins and needles to get to that ultrasound. His peace continued to flood our souls, even as our emotions would rise and fall—plunge, even. Our prayer was for God's peace to resonate through our whole family during this journey, and that others would SEE that supernatural peace and desire to know the Prince of Peace on a personal level.

ෆ𝕏øෑ𝕏ฌෆ𝕏øෑ𝕏ฌ

Written September 29, 2016.

Yesterday I learned a few things…

- *It is much, MUCH harder to share difficult news with people in person than it is over the phone or computer.*
- *You can get a much-needed nap…but when you wake up, nothing has really changed.*
- *The words "funeral arrangements" have no business being a part of a discussion with your spouse about a coming baby. In light of eternity, Death does not have the victory, but here on earth, that grave surely does have a sting. Curse you, Satan.*

☙❧☙☙☙❧☙☙

The following days and weeks were spent in a fog. It was so bizarre to live with such a sense of loss that was all too real. And yet Verity was still very much alive. I felt her movements more and more each day. I have marveled over the years at how wondrous it is to feel a human being growing and taking shape within my own body—I never, ever got over those fluttery kicks that later become stronger jabs and sharp pokes. Whether it is the first or the ninth baby, it is an indescribable feeling.

And feeling a live, wiggly baby, while not knowing just how long she might be alive, is such a strange, strange place emotionally and mentally.

There is life…and death…all in one thought.

It was exhausting.

I slept, but not really: I was in a seemingly endless state of weariness that numbed the senses even as it sharpened emotion.

I forgot, but not really: I immersed myself in necessary activities (homeschooling and home management after a fashion), and when that time of focus ended, I remembered reality once again.

And it hurt.

This was life in our new normal, a "normal" that stretched before us indefinitely. We continued with our routine as much as possible, for there is comfort and security in the familiar, especially where children are concerned. Yet we had to keep giving ourselves and each other grace upon grace, for who can function in a fog?

Life in this fog revealed strange yet beautiful paradoxes.

Joy in sadness.

Peace with uncertainty.

Physical fatigue, spiritual rest.

I cried. A lot. But sometimes I laughed. And I wondered, always, in the back of my mind, how in the world I would keep from losing my mind if I had to experience losing this child.

CREDEDCROSEDEDCR

The day it was confirmed that our baby girl had Trisomy 18, I signed up as a volunteer for a one-hour shift during the 40 Days for Life campaign. This was to be a prayer vigil, standing peacefully in front of a local Planned Parenthood.

From the time I was a young teen, I have always been passionately pro-life. My stance has never changed—however, I humbly admit my perspective of "the other side" has morphed from one consisting entirely of critical judgment to one full of compassion, grace, and mercy. While I still could never condone abortion, friendships with dear friends who have experienced an abortion have helped me gain a small understanding of the turmoil before, during, and after the traumatic event.

Now I was actually carrying a child in my womb with "abnormalities," the kind that leave some mothers feeling a desperate sort of grief, perhaps a feeling that there really is no other option for them other than to abort. And my heart ached for them in a different way than ever before. From the beginning of our journey with Verity, we asserted that abortion was not ever an option for us, because we stand on the truth of God's Word, truth that teaches all humans are created in the image of God (Genesis 1:27); that we are all fearfully and wonderfully made (Psalm 139); that God knew us before we were even conceived (Jeremiah 1:5); that God has plans for us that reach into eternity (Ephesians 2:8-10).

Because we know the truth, it has set us free from fear and anxiety. This is not to say we do not grieve or feel pain or sadness; on the contrary, we feel and grieve deeply. Agonizingly. During these days and weeks following our diagnosis, my husband and I wept together during our prayer times as we shared some of our fears with each other.

But wait—didn't you say you were free from fear?!

Yes. We are free from the fear that paralyzes, fear that hinders us from moving forward in faith. *God has not given us a spirit of fear, but a spirit of love, of power, and of a sound mind (2 Timothy 1:7).*

God's truth gives us joy that can't be explained; peace that is beyond understanding; and hope that does not disappoint. I am thankful beyond words for truth.

And I have considered what the ramifications would be for me, for my family, for Baby Verity...if I did not know truth.

If all I had was a diagnosis...

If all I knew were the statistics...

If my only counsel were to consider what was best for *me* in the here and now...

What would I do? What would I choose?

I couldn't even imagine. I reflected on these thoughts as I stood with three of my children while cold wind whipped about our faces, smiling and praying blessings over drivers who honked and waved as well as those who shouted obscenities. We prayed God would reveal truth to those who are searching as well as to those who think they know it all. We prayed God's people would reach out with love and compassion to those who are in desperate circumstances as well as to those who simply feel inconvenienced.

That day...today...and always...I stand for life.

Because I have carried precious life within me.

Because I enjoy the beauty of life on earth.

And because through Jesus I have the gift of eternal life.

"For God so loved the world that He gave His one and only Son, that whoever believes in Him shall not perish but have eternal life." John 3:16

CRITOCRITO

I tucked Kenna in bed one evening and talked, at her request, about her baby sister.

"Mom, the other night I saw Verity."

"What do you mean, sweetie?"

"I saw her, Mom! She had long, dark hair, and she was running!"

"Oh, honey." I didn't know what to say. Surely my nine-year-old could understand this wasn't possible. "You must have had a dream."

"No, Mom. I looked right over there"—she pointed to a spot in her room—"and I watched her. I saw her dark hair flowing."

My heart sank. I couldn't voice my thoughts, that my daughter must have seen a vision of her sister, healed and whole and running in heaven. For that, I was sure, was the only way this dream would ever come true.

CRITOCRITO

We had another ultrasound a month after the first one, which had not yielded good visibility for Verity's heart. I was so looking forward to getting another glimpse of our baby girl, whose movements grow increasingly stronger day by day. I was also anticipating some answers—something, anything—that might help us prepare for what Verity would need, what she would be like, upon her arrival.

Verity was in the same face-down position as during the previous ultrasound, but her increased growth allowed much better visibility for the tech whose priority was to get good shots and measurements of her heart and profile. Aside from her little feet turning inward and the clenched hands, both typical of Trisomy 18, everything looked so beautifully normal to us as parents. Our technician was kind and talkative and able to complete her tasks quickly. Before long we heard the following report from the doctor:

- The baby's heart looks very normal—this was an immense relief and an answer to prayer, as many T18 babies have heart issues.
- There was no sign of a cleft lip (which could indicate a cleft palate but is not something that can be determined by ultrasound). Again, cause for celebration. No matter what this precious baby's appearance, I knew I would see her as beautiful; however, one of my prayers from the beginning was for our other children to feel connected to and not repulsed by their baby sister. Additionally, it gave me hope that perhaps I would even be able to nurse Verity.

- Despite slowed growth being typical of T18 babies, Verity was of an average weight for a baby at 22 weeks gestation (about a pound).
- The doctor could see no other physical concerns that were not already noted in the previous screening. Again, reason to praise the Lord!

Based on this assessment, Dr. B even questioned the need for Verity to be in the NICU[11], assuming she arrived close enough to her due date and was delivered without complications. She also suggested that whether I chose to do a C-section delivery or not would not make any difference. At first I thought this was encouraging news, but then I began to realize the doctor didn't think it would make a difference because *she wasn't invested in the outcome.*

Dr. B asked us some questions we could not really answer, mostly because it seemed so many of those answers would have had to begin with the words, "It depends..." I don't remember all of the questions, but I do remember phrases like *hospice care, medical interventions,* and *ethical decisions.* As Ted and I stared blankly at each other throughout these queries, it became all too obvious that, despite the research we had done, we simply did not have enough information to equip us for the wide range of possibilities ahead of us.

Despite hearing all this, we left somehow feeling as if we knew even less than we did before the ultrasound. And it all felt like a chasing after the wind. We

---

[11] Neonatal Intensive Care Unit

had some answers, a few precious facts to hold onto. But somehow they weren't enough. They weren't what I was looking for. Which begged the question...what exactly WAS I looking for...longing for?

Traffic and miles of highways gave me plenty of time alone in the car to think and pray as I headed home while Ted returned to work. Why was I feeling so emotional? What was my problem? The news about Verity had all been good—so many answers to specific prayers. And truly, I was grateful for the good report.

Anger.

Seemingly out of nowhere, a rage roiled inside of me, even as I felt the crushing weight of despondency. And it took shape more quickly than the words I tried to form in prayer.

Anger at the clinical approach and unhelpful explanations from the doctor regarding the ultrasound.

Anger at her constant referral to our baby girl as *it* instead of *she* or *her*.

Anger at feeling helpless and uncertain after being on the receiving end of a storm of questions—and this from a doctor who seemed determined to make us see the futility of preserving or prolonging the life of our child.

And I was angry at having to be in the position of waiting...interminable waiting...instead of planning. Don't we do enough *waiting* as a military family?? Always waiting, waiting, waiting, uncertain about what is coming next. And at this time, we were also *waiting* for specific leading from God—to retire after 20 years or not? Before Verity's T18 diagnosis, we felt a peace about staying on active duty. But now we were *waiting* for that next assignment. Yet everything seemed extraordinarily more complicated. Would we be moving to our next duty location as a family of 11 with a special-needs baby...or as a family of 10 grieving the loss of a child, a sibling?

And fear. Oh, the fear.

It was ugly. Many days I didn't have time for fear; other days it simply wasn't a part of my life because *life* is too full of God's joy and peace. When I lived in worship, walking by faith instead of by sight, purposefully engaged in what God called me to do, fear was not a factor.

But. Feelings have a mind of their own, don't they? And so fear washed over me inexplicably, even as I experienced the precious peace that never truly leaves but somehow seems quiet in those moments of crashing, frightful waves.

I sat in our driveway after a long afternoon of medical talk, errands, driving, thinking, and praying. I sat quite awhile, overcome by these powerful emotions that I hated to admit I had. Didn't I trust God? Didn't I take Him at His word? Hadn't He proved Himself loving and good and faithful no matter what my circumstances?

Yes. All that is true. Truth is truth, regardless of feelings. But what I was feeling was also real.

I arrived home from this much anticipated appointment feeling battered and bruised emotionally. From anger so powerful it left me shaking in the driveway to gut-wrenching fear that ripped at my heart when I least expected it, I felt pummeled even as I strove to tread water amidst the "smaller" waves of sadness and confusion. In searching for tangible answers to my Trisomy 18 questions, I only found more uncertainty.

"On Christ the solid Rock I stand,
All other ground is sinking sand...all other ground
is sinking sand..."

For now we see through a glass, darkly; but then face to face: now I know in part; but then shall I know even as also I am known. (1 Corinthians 13:12, KJV)

I have told our kids multiple times that our God is big enough to handle questions and doubts. I don't want to serve a God I fully understand—how would He then be God?! I will never have things figured out this side of heaven. I will continue to wrestle. But like Jacob, I won't let go until He blesses me.[12]

Why, my soul, are you downcast?
Why so disturbed within me?
Put your hope in God,
for I will yet praise him,
my Savior and my God.
Psalm 42:11

I clung to the truth in this verse, a hopeful note, a note of confidence in my Savior and my God. Yet it wouldn't be honest to say my faith allowed me to completely set aside my disturbed feelings. Specific fears continued to haunt me as time marched toward our due

---

[12] Genesis 32:22-32

date and all the uncertainty it entailed. Lord willing, I will bare it all; this isn't my story, but His. My deepest desire is to honor God, and even though some of the sharing will be painful and ugly, I think that just as I had to wrestle with the downcast, disturbed parts of me in order to get to that place of hope and praise, I also have to reveal that struggle so that—Lord willing—others will also put their hope in God.

CRStÐ§ÐCRCRStÐ§ÐCR

We had left the medical center with another appointment scheduled for the following week: a consultation with the genetic counselor as well as a doctor from the NICU. The idea was for these professionals to help us think through the "what ifs," and even to know what exactly some of those "what ifs" might be.

Our first meeting was with the genetic counselor whom we met the day of the diagnostic ultrasound for Verity. This was a good and productive meeting. Sara was very well prepared and gave us a lot of positive information about babies and children with Trisomy 18. Based on our ultrasound findings thus far, Sara thought Verity had a good chance of survival. Obviously there were no guarantees, and there are often problems that ultrasounds miss, but the overall picture thus far showed us that she seemed to have a "head start," so to speak: if any baby were to have a positive outlook with this diagnosis, our Verity would seem to be one who might enter the world ready to fight the good fight.

Sara's whole demeanor was extremely positive and encouraging. She gave us the full story of the hopeful end of the spectrum, even though we were all fully aware of the grim statistics. In her words, we would get enough of the negative from plenty of other sources, so she wanted to focus on things that would be helpful for us in the event that we were able to bring Verity home from the hospital.

Our next meeting was with the head neonatologist at the university hospital where I would deliver. I was looking forward to hearing about the measures our medical team would naturally take at the event of an expected Trisomy 18 birth. I was caught completely off guard when nearly the first thing out of his mouth was something about dealing with a "retarded" child. He seemingly excused his use of that term by explaining that he grew up with a "mentally retarded sister." Over the course of our meeting—which was less a conversation than it was me listening in stunned silence—I gleaned some information that gave a bit of insight into his wording and overall lack of understanding or compassion for our family's situation.

This doctor's sister did not get enough oxygen at birth, and so she lived her 19 years with a mental handicap. This apparently took a toll on him personally and presumably on his other family members; he spent much of our brief time together talking about the importance of "buy-in" from the whole family, because when there is a baby/child with these kinds of needs, everybody must pitch in and help. And while I don't disagree with that, I believe our family already had a much different (and healthier) perspective. Our kids have always understood that we have to work hard together and serve one another in order for things to run halfway smoothly! If we want to have fun together, we need to work together to create the time and space for those times to happen. But life in general involves putting others' interests and needs ahead of our own, especially for those who take Jesus's commands seriously. We don't always do this with humble, Christ-like attitudes, but still, we do have this basic understanding from Scripture and work hard to teach it to our children.

The man continued. Verity would undoubtedly live what he considered a "futile" life (a word he used with alarming frequency). And a life such as this would take a toll on the whole family. According to him, living with a developmentally disabled person is a strain physically, mentally, emotionally, and financially.

Somehow, in between all of these negative opinions, I managed to glean actual medical information, such as the fact that the staff would do basic, necessary measures such as resuscitation, assisting with baby's breathing, giving feeding help, and so on, unless we instructed them not to do these things (which for us obviously wasn't an option). In any case, the doctor made it pretty clear what he thought about giving additional support measures to a child like ours. *"Futile."* I learned much later that this doctor did not speak for the majority of the staff—not in the least—but at the time his negativity completely overwhelmed me.

I'm sure folks reading this are thinking, "Why didn't you tell him off?!" And truly, as I drove home, shaking with anger and wiping away tears, I thought of a boatload of things I could have or should have said. But perhaps you've been in a similar situation where you felt punched in the gut—caught completely unaware, listening to someone say things so far removed from what you expected to hear, that you couldn't even formulate words in your own brain, let alone speak them.

I did wrap up the meeting sooner rather than later, and as I stood and headed toward the door, I was stunned yet again when he asked me, "This is your last child, I hope?" He then went on to ask what my "religious affiliation" was.

Good grief.

I was as polite as I could be and simply pray that the parting words I left with him will speak volumes of truth to his heart as long as he lives. No matter how long Verity's life span, she was *already* a blessing and a gift, even in my womb with this unexpected diagnosis. She is not a mistake. Her life is not futile. As her family, we may have had fears and doubts about our abilities to care for whatever her unique needs were going to be, but we never doubted God's beauty and purpose in all things and that He would glorify Himself through this child.

CRISORISCRISOSISCR

My anger at the way the neonatologist spoke to me that day served a holy purpose: it raised the mama bear inside of me and set me to researching with determined vigor. If this was the attitude of the world toward our baby, then it was up to us to advocate for her. I read research articles and joined online Trisomy parent groups, reading posts and comments and making all kinds of notes.

One of the most startling discoveries I made seemed backwards—statistically speaking, a prenatal Trisomy diagnosis actually hurts a child's chances of survival compared to a postnatal diagnosis. And yet, when I consider the words of the neonatologist, it completely makes sense. Most parents, especially those facing a devastating diagnosis, have been conditioned to trust health care professionals. However, sometimes the information they receive may actually be outdated, perhaps because the medical professionals are relying on grim statistics that ignore (or are ignorant of) any positive outcomes. And as I experienced, it is entirely possible that sometimes the information coming to parents has already been pre-filtered through the lenses of a health care professional's personal beliefs. Do you see the importance of this? Parents, already feeling fragile and even devastated because of an unexpected diagnosis, must make decisions regarding the life and viability of their child based on prejudice, faulty statistics, and a false narrative! Under this influence, parents who don't know anything better than what they have been told may accept and and act on these sentiments. This could cause them to make choices that will negatively impact the outcome of a vulnerable and precious life!

It was heartbreaking to me to find in my research that in many cases, parents prepared for the worst. They were not encouraged by those whom they trusted with their baby's well-being to take basic, life-saving measures given automatically to babies who were born without any diagnosis whatsoever. I was so grateful we had the opportunity to turn this story around. Ted and I completely rejected the negative narrative presented to us at the beginning of this Trisomy journey. Our prenatal diagnosis had given us time to process an extraordinary amount of information in a relatively short amount of time. What we were learning equipped us to be the best advocates possible for our daughter.

And yet, I was struggling. As the days crawled by one by one, slowly approaching our due date of February 25, 2017, I felt myself being torn up more and more inside.

 CB೮೮ಣ೮೮ಣ

Written in my prayer journal November 1, 2016:

Job 30:16-22 [part of my assigned daily Scripture reading] seems so real to me today.

"And now my soul is poured out within me; days of affliction have taken hold of me. The night racks my bones, and the pain that gnaws me takes no rest. With great force my garment is disfigured; it binds about me

like the collar of my tunic. [My non-academic paraphrase: I feel as if I'm choking.] *God has cast me into the mire, and I have become like dust and ashes. I cry to you for help and you do not answer me; I stand, and you only look at me. You have turned cruel to me; with the might of your hand you persecute me. You lift me up on the wind, you make me ride on it, and you toss me about in the roar of the storm."*

God...this heaviness. I can't bear it. Help me. I have no right to ask for your help, no right at all on my own merit. You know the depths of my heart: the ugliness. Selfishness. Resentment. Fear. Feeling resigned to a burden I may carry for...who knows how long? As awful, as ugly as it is, I can't be anything other than completely naked before you. After wrestling and somewhat coming to terms with the real possibility that our baby may die...I find myself now completely terrified that...

...she might live.

Devastating. I'm devastated to face that ugliness inside me. I'm ashamed of what it reveals about me. I'm sorry to say that my heart isn't always in line with what I know is true...

Your grace is sufficient.
Your power is perfect in my weakness.
Your mercies are new every morning.
Your faithfulness is unending.
Your steadfast love never fails.
You carry all my burdens.
You give joy in the morning.

You work all things for good.

You will accomplish your purposes.

You are refining us and making us more like you.

What can I say? You've never "listened" to me when I've cried out, "ENOUGH! I can't take any more!" My hands were more than full when Kenna came along! And though I can't imagine life without our precious Kenna, Lucan, Zaden, Seanin, and Rhema, I AM FULL. OVERWHELMED.

I know special-needs families love their children. Life revolves around serving these vulnerable, precious ones, and they wouldn't trade it for anything. I see, hear, feel the love as they talk or type about their children. I already love Verity, and I wouldn't trade this for my own plans—we all know that your plans and ways are much higher than ours. I know. I know. I KNOW.

But.

Sigh.

Someday maybe I won't focus on the but. *Today is not that day. Today I look ahead and see real possibility of a life centered around medical appointments and special equipment for our special girl. I see lack of sleep, lack of order, lack of energy for my marriage and our other kids—our eight other precious kids whom YOU have given to us. Certainly no room for activities outside my home. Sure, I also see a lot of growth and compassion and love. But. (There's that word again.) It comes with a huge dose of exhaustion and ever-present concern.*

And I am utterly, completely overwhelmed.

So there it was—the raw, ugly truth. While my mama bear instinct had kicked in and I was already fighting for our unborn baby to have her best possible chance at life, I was also struggling with the thought of having a special-needs child to care for along with the rest of our big family. Once again I felt I was straddling seemingly incompatible feelings.

The new year of 2017 dawned for us with complete uncertainty. It also included a widening circle of acquaintances within the Trisomy community. I peeked in on their daily joys and struggles online. All too often, though, we learned of the loss of one of these little ones, whether in utero or after a life well loved outside the womb. I shed many tears over babies and children I would never meet. I didn't even know these people personally, and yet we were connected because of a diagnosis. The beauty and fragility of the lives of our babies connected us in both encouraging and heart-breaking ways.

What did this new year hold for us? For Verity? Would we make it to her due date or even beyond? There were so many more questions than answers—which is a testimony to how outdated much of the available information about this diagnosis really was at that time. Our early research had us assuming we would be burying Verity shortly after birth. But through the journey, we learned enough to realize that we would likely need to answer different questions, such as:

- What will be the best way to help Verity breathe if, like many other T18 babies, she needs respiratory support?
- What kind of feeding support will we need to give her?
- How tiny will she be? Will preemie outfits work?
- What kinds of monitoring will we need to learn?

And looming over it all...would Verity be with us when we moved to our next location? Or would we have to say goodbye to her, laying her to rest before packing up and starting over somewhere else?

It was too exhausting, too depressing to wonder what our lives would look like in the coming months. As much as we know God has a plan and purpose for all of this, as much as we acknowledge His power, His sovereignty, His love—this walk of faith was the hardest thing I had ever done. There were times when answers simply were not available, times when I knew Truth but couldn't feel it. Times when I was in God's Word and yet felt crushed, overwhelmed, and discouraged. Times when I sat in prayer, yet could say absolutely nothing.

The dreary, colorless days of January reflected what I experienced as an emotional season of winter. I longed for spring. New life. New hope. The fact that Verity was due toward the end of winter did not escape me. I was tired of tracing trails of thoughts I had never before had to follow. This winter was hard, dark, depressing and even oppressing at times.

But we do not grieve as those who have no hope (1 Thessalonians 4:13). And we encourage one another (verse 18)—or allow ourselves to be encouraged—by the words of truth.

"Shall we receive good from God, and shall we not receive evil?" Job 2:10

"In the day of prosperity be joyful, and in the day of adversity consider: God has made the one as well as the other..." Ecclesiastes 7:14

I am grateful for an eternal, unchanging God, my Rock in tumultuous, changing circumstances. I am grateful He not only hears my cries...He also knows and understands my pain and confusion.

"Since then we have a great high priest who has passed through the heavens, Jesus, the Son of God, let us hold fast our confession. For we do not have a high priest who is unable to sympathize with our weaknesses, but one who in every respect has been tempted as we are, yet without sin. Let us then with confidence draw near to the throne of grace, that we may receive mercy and find grace to help us in time of need." Hebrews 4:14-16

During this difficult season of uncertainty, I was ever so grateful for loved ones who allow me the freedom to cry and rant and wallow in the pain and difficulty of fear and uncertainty—and yet gently reminded me (or prayed for the Holy Spirit to remind me!) that God would use every facet of this journey in order to conform us to the likeness of Jesus and to bring Him eternal glory.

I was ever so grateful for the privilege of sitting in the presence of a holy God, unafraid and unashamed to spill out my true thoughts and feelings. And I was grateful for His love that would never let me go. Even when I'm angry and acting and feeling unlovable, He still holds me close.

We walk by faith, not by sight...we walk by faith, not by feelings. Thank God for the gift of faith! And thank God for the gift of spring. For it always comes. We appreciate the warmth, the sunshine, and the signs of new life all the more because of the cold, dark days of winter.

Whatever was going to happen with Verity...we knew the truth. And the truth sets us free and allows us to rejoice in the new life God has given us: literal life on earth as we waited to bring forth another child into this world, but even more important, eternal life with Him, a life that will make everything on earth fade away as we step out of the darkness of winter and into everlasting spring.

Weeping may tarry for the night, but joy comes with the morning...You have turned for me my mourning into dancing; you have loosed my sackcloth and clothed me with gladness, that my glory may sing your praise and not be silent. O LORD my God, I will give thanks to you forever! Psalm 30:5b, 11-12

☙❧❧☙☙❧❧☙

We arrived at the labor and delivery ward at 1:00 a.m. on February 28, 2017. I was already dilated 6cm when we arrived, and with Verity being small, we anticipated a fairly quick delivery. It felt surreal actually being in labor after waiting and wondering for what had seemed like an eternity. The fact that it happened in the middle of the night only added to the dream-like quality of the whole experience. Still, I appreciated the calm and the quiet: all I felt was peace. Overwhelming peace.

As per my birth plan, we requested an epidural so in case something happened and Verity ended up in distress, I would be alert for an emergency C-section. The contractions were so minimally uncomfortable; honestly, it was the easiest labor I've had, other than the fact I was just so tired from being awake all day.

One of the blessings and answers to my prayers for Verity's delivery was that my favorite doctor (who had delivered another Trisomy 18 baby recently) was on duty that night. He ended up having to do some maneuvering once my labor had come to a halt: Verity was transverse! But the manipulation worked. Within minutes we were ready to have a baby!

Easiest delivery ever from that point on: I pushed carefully a little at a time and there she was, all beautiful and dark-haired and perfect. I got to cuddle her on my chest for a few precious minutes while time stood still and I wept tears of joy unlike any I've shed over my other babies—and I've cried at seeing each precious face, because the miracle of life is something we never get over, nor should we. But this living, breathing, five-pound, three-ounce baby girl was the definition of a miracle for me in that indescribable span of time. Here she was. So loved. So cherished. All the fears I secretly harbored about whether I could possibly love a "different" child as much as I loved my other children completely melted away. I loved her with all my heart. I could tell Ted felt the same as I watched him cut the umbilical cord, and big sister Charis also looked on with love written all over her face. We regretfully agreed after a short while that we needed to let Verity go with the NICU team. Even love-filled eyes couldn't deny she was turning gray.

It was time to determine what exactly Verity's immediate needs were and what the team could determine about her future needs. Clearly she had to have respiratory support, but we were thrilled when the CPAP[13] mask was removed within the first 24 hours and she moved to room oxygen through a nasal cannula. Even more astonishing was seeing her come off oxygen altogether on day five and having her do so well.

Apnea can cause major problems with Trisomy babies, but thankfully for us, nothing thus far indicated Verity had any of these issues. I took courage every time I looked at her monitors and saw such regularity— perfect little heartbeat, high oxygen saturations, rhythmic breathing. That changed when she was angry, but even hearing her lusty cries made me smile instead of panic. Verity quickly became known as a little fighter amongst all her nurses.

Next: feedings. We figured Verity would need help eating, as almost all Trisomy babies do. She got an IV right away, followed by gavage feedings (through a tube, first in her mouth and later through her nostril). We were

---

[13] Continuous Positive Airway Pressure, a machine that sends a constant flow of pressure to the throat to ensure the airway stays open.

given a bottle of donor milk for her to use until I was able to pump enough to establish my own supply. Feeding amounts steadily increased, and she tolerated it all very well. She had no problems eliminating, which was another answer to prayer.

I was hopeful Verity might be able to nurse (I had read of some T18 babies who did). She latched and sucked several times during different attempts, so while we never really had any sustained suck-and-swallow action, there were indicators that this was possible. We did not do an official swallow evaluation until some weeks later.

We had requested in our birth plan to have a brain scan done, and that was done the day of her birth. Everything looked fantastic!

We had also requested an echocardiogram[14], even though careful examination of her heart during the prime viewing period of my pregnancy indicated that she had no heart issues. It wasn't terribly surprising but was still rather discouraging to learn that there were, in fact, heart issues. Verity had three ventricular septal defects (VSDs, holes in the lower chamber of her heart). Two of them were small, and the cardiologist thought they might very well resolve on their own. The third, however, was large enough that the doctor thought Verity would require heart surgery before age one. This is very common for Trisomy babies, and we were grateful to be in a "Trisomy friendly" hospital where we knew Verity would get the care any other child would receive. Her

---

[14] A graphic outline of the heart's movement.

diagnosis would not be a factor in determining the best course of action for her.

All of Verity's positive (and fast) progress made us wonder if perhaps instead of full Trisomy 18, she might actually have partial or mosaic Trisomy 18. What is the difference?

Full Trisomy 18 is the most common type. In full Trisomy, the extra chromosome occurs in every cell in the baby's body. This type of trisomy is not hereditary. It is not due to anything the parents did or did not do—either before or during pregnancy. Nor, I might add, is it because of the age of the mother.

Partial trisomies are very rare and occur when only part of an extra chromosome is present. Affected people have two copies of chromosome 18, plus a "partial" piece of extra material from chromosome 18.

Mosaic trisomy is also very rare. It occurs when the extra chromosome is present in some but not all of the cells of the body. Like full Trisomy 18, mosaic Trisomy is not inherited and is a random occurrence that takes place during cell division.

At the time I was researching this syndrome, there was a fairly prevalent idea floating around in Trisomy communities, and that was if a child had the mosaic form, he or she would fare better developmentally. I suppose the theory is that since not all of the cells are affected, it leaves room for more "normal" growth and behaviors. But from my unofficial research and observations, I have come to the conclusion that whether a person has full or mosaic Trisomy 18 really is not the issue. Whether or not an affected individual is given every opportunity to grow and thrive, receiving whatever kind of support is necessary for that individual's unique needs—*this* is a more dependable indicator for whether a Trisomy 18 person will thrive.

We didn't know exactly what lay ahead of us now that Verity lived outside my womb. But we were prepared to do whatever was necessary to love and care for this tiny human God had so graciously entrusted to us.

For if we didn't fully understand it before she entered the world, by now it was clear that Verity was indeed God's gift to us: a gift in Trisomy 18 packaging.

C820808CR0808080808

We spent 18 days in the NICU. It was a blur of visitors and medical personnel. Every day we learned something different about how to take care of Verity. By the time we were cleared for discharge, we knew how to operate her feeding pump, a suction machine, and a pulse oximeter[15]. Looking at the boxes with all of the medical supplies, I felt slightly overwhelmed. Were they really going to let us go home with this fragile, needy, little human? I reminded myself that these machines represented life for Verity. We had no way of knowing how long we would need them or whether we would need to learn about other equipment at a later date. For now, we knew enough to walk the next few steps down the road.

---

[15] A device that measures the oxygen level of the blood.

During my NICU stint with Verity, it became clear that being Verity's mom was a full-time job. I expected a huge learning curve and knew it had to get easier after giving everything some time. I fully believe God allowed me to experience such dramatic feeding difficulties with Zaden and Rhema to help prepare me for this journey. I had hoped that eventually Verity could nurse, but in the meantime, I was committed to pumping and at least providing her with the nourishment I had given her siblings. Simply keeping Verity alive was going to require intense time, effort, and energy on not only my part but also the rest of the family's as well.

Despite the qualms, we had reasons aplenty to rejoice. Not only were we bringing home our very-much-alive baby girl, but we had also learned a few days prior that an updated echocardiogram showed the large VSD was already closing—Verity was not going to need heart surgery after all! What a miracle and blessing! I had texted my friend and prayer partner the news, and she responded, "Yesterday in children's church Zaden asked for prayer for Verity to be here on earth for a long time. We prayed that her heart would heal. Prayers of children I think avail much."

Indeed! Why do I marvel at all...I had wondered why God hadn't shown us via ultrasound the issues with Verity's heart so that we would know about that before she was born. Now I think what a blessing it is that we didn't know; surely it would have only added to the mental and emotional burdens we already carried throughout my pregnancy.

We praised and thanked God for so many answered prayers, realizing that He is good no matter what our circumstances. I have wept with parents whose little ones were *not* healed, or who were *not* born alive. I didn't understand then, nor will I ever understand this side of heaven, why God allowed our little Verity to live and (so far) thrive with such a positive potential outlook when so many other sweet children have had parents fighting for and with them and yet had to say goodbye all too soon.

Chapter 16

Year One

It was a relief to finally be home and begin working toward a new family normal. The first night we startled to the sound of the pulse oximeter beeping loudly during a few de-satting episodes (when Verity's oxygen saturations dropped below normal range). The second night we were in the emergency room after Verity's NG (nasogastric) tube came out of her nose and needed to be put in again, which required an X-ray to ensure proper placement. Never a dull moment!

The weeks that followed involved numerous medical assessments and specialty appointments. Verity got her first set of casts for clubfoot correction when she was only six weeks old, and we had weekly castings for about a month before her first surgery, a tendon release of both Achilles' tendons, followed by another set of casts.

There was a swallow study, another cardio assessment, an upper GI series[16], and an extensive hearing test since Verity did not pass her newborn screening. There were well-child check-ups and trips to the emergency room to get the NG placed properly after it either had come out or gotten clogged.

When people have medical problems that prevent them from being able to take adequate nutrition by mouth, they may opt to have a gastrostomy tube (also called a G-tube) placed. We decided to schedule surgery when Verity was two months old for her to receive one of these tubes. During a procedure lasting less than an hour, the surgeon inserted the G-tube through the abdomen so she could receive nutrition directly into her stomach. Since it was clear Verity would have difficulty eating for at least the foreseeable future, this was one way to make sure she would get the fluid and calories she needed to grow. We were not at all sad to say goodbye to the NG tube that had given us so many problems and panic attacks! The G-tube was a more permanent solution allowing nourishment to flow directly into Verity's belly. I had given up the idea of nursing our last baby; the unique shape of her mouth and palate, plus her difficulty sucking and swallowing, meant she could not possibly eat enough to sustain herself let alone grow. But she was growing! Slowly but surely!

---

[16] A procedure in which a doctor uses x-rays, fluoroscopy, and a chalky liquid called barium to view the upper GI tract.

On June 28, 2017, Ted and I celebrated 20 years of marriage. This also happened to be Verity's four-month birthday. It's impossible to look back over the years and not see God's hand at work in our lives. And He continued to work on our behalf. The Air Force sent Ted to Colorado Springs for his next assignment. We could hardly believe we were coming HOME, home to the mountains and this gorgeous state we both loved so much. My heart soared as we drove into the city and moved into our beautiful rental home overlooking the Front Range and the iconic Air Force Academy chapel.

Moving is always so exhausting—it's much more work than you ever remember. Kind of like labor, actually. You forget how painful it is until you're in the middle of the next time around! The more kids we added to our family, the more arduous this whole moving process had become. And having Verity added a whole new level of difficulty. Now we needed to start from scratch with her medical care, establishing baselines as well as continuing care (such as her clubfoot correction, which had moved on to the boots-and-bar phase, a special brace she needed to wear 23 hours a day). There were truckloads of paperwork and countless phone calls to make or answer. On top of all of that, moving to the high altitude had contributed to a seemingly new issue: Verity had reflux so badly that she was experiencing violent vomiting episodes multiple times a day. We used the suction machine far more than we ever had before the move, and we lived in terror that she might aspirate. Additionally, the child did not sleep. I'm not talking about typical infant nighttime waking. I mean she never truly slept at all. Literally every 10-15 minutes, all night long, Verity would wake, fuss, and cry. We would do what we could to help her, doze off, and start all over again eight minutes later. Even in the daytime we were lucky if she napped five or ten minutes once or twice a day.

Truly, it's a miracle we made it through those months of severe sleep deprivation. I can't explain how we did it except by the grace of God. I now have insight into why so many marriage relationships crumble when a special-needs child is added to the family dynamics. I have thanked the Lord over and over for a strong marriage, but don't think for one second that this was easy for us. Lack of sleep leads to lack of communication, especially when a couple is passing the torch at night in order to get at least three or four uninterrupted hours of rest. And in addition to the difficulty communicating is the all-around strenuous task of simply living and thinking. You shift into survival mode, and it isn't pretty. I had thought the year we had Arden, when we had three children three years old and under, was a blur. But this...this was on a whole different level.

Not surprisingly, Ted and I both struggled with anxiety and depression. I clung to daily time in the Word, even when I didn't feel like it—I journaled prayers of anger, sadness, and despair. Once again I turned to my essential oils, setting reminders on my phone to apply them several times a day. I had to avoid the abyss that

142

threatened to swallow me. I didn't know it was possible to experience so many emotions without exploding, but here they were, oozing out every way I turned.

I still struggled with fear of the unknown, for we had traded the uncertainty of whether Verity would be born alive for the uncertainty of exactly how long she would be with us. I spent way too much time during that first year holding my breath, halfway expecting her to die at any moment.

And guilt was a constant companion, because if I struggled this much, clearly (I thought) I must not fully appreciate the many blessings surrounding me. Plenty of families would have given everything to have even the most difficult days with their loved ones again. Why couldn't I just be grateful we had Verity with us instead of feeling so stressed out all the time?

More guilt when I thought about my other children and teens. The plates I tried to keep spinning were crashing all around me—homeschool my kids? Who was I kidding? I could barely keep everyone fed, including the tiniest one in the mix. I pumped every three hours almost around the clock (I was awake at night anyway, so why not?!) and had to be on alert for the little signs that preceded emesis...and sometimes it happened without warning. One day when Verity began vomiting copious amounts, I watched with a mixture of sadness and pride as two-year-old Rhema shouted, "I'll get a burp cloth!" and tossed one in my direction before trying to lug the suction machine to me as well. She didn't know life could be any other way than it was with our Verity.

I've never had trouble making friends—I'm extroverted enough that I find it fun to get to know other people. But the transition to Colorado Springs seemed more difficult for me, and understandably so. Going out of the house was a Herculean task, so we mostly just went to church and medical appointments. Everyone we met was so very kind, and our church family especially took an interest in learning about Verity and prayed much for her and our family. It warmed my heart to watch them fall in love with our wee babe. But somewhere along the way I began to feel known simply as "Verity's mom." Everybody loves Verity and wants to know how she's doing, so naturally they ask me. Not as many folks ask how Mama is doing. And many days, she's the one who is falling apart inside. I experienced sadness and loneliness like never before. I had no idea how isolating the life of a special-needs parent truly is. It gave me tremendous insight into the everyday lives of people I hadn't known all that well before I entered their world.

I even felt sad and lonely in my own home, in my own dining room and bedroom. Not only did Ted and I hardly ever sleep at the same time, but it was pretty much impossible to ever be alone (and coherent enough) to have meaningful conversation. We couldn't leave Verity with anyone, so even though our teens did a fine job of babysitting their younger siblings when needed, there certainly was never any opportunity for date nights.

When Verity was eight months old, the Lord sent some rays of sunshine from heaven in the form of our home health care agency. It had never occurred to me that we could qualify to receive in-home care for Verity, but the early intervention program in our area got the ball rolling. We had been receiving weekly physical and occupational therapy visits for about two months, which was also a blessing. And now we would have a nurse in our home 40 hours a week, a professional whose sole job would be to take care of Verity.

Although our first nurse was only with us about three months, she helped us make this transition so beautifully. I finally stopped feeling guilty that I wasn't the one taking care of Verity all the time anymore. Instead, I poured out time and what little energy I had into my other kids, who had bravely and gallantly done so much on their own during those months I kept Verity all but glued to my side, too paranoid to leave her.

I suppose it could have been awkward, allowing a near stranger to come into our house and work around the rest of us while we went through our daily chores and routines. But somehow it seemed very natural, and I thanked God every day for this saving grace. Our nurse fell in love with Verity and also took time to learn the rest of our kids' names, interacting with them as sweetly and graciously as she did with her client. I don't know how we would have continued homeschooling if it hadn't been for our nurse! We have since experienced a few other transitions, but every nurse our home health agency has sent us has been such a perfect fit for our family at the time. They truly are part of our family, and we couldn't imagine things any other way.

Another blessing came to us in the form of a friend from church. Edie asked us if we could teach her how to take care of Verity so that she could come to our house once a week and stay overnight, allowing Ted and me to get some uninterrupted sleep. I was stunned—I could hardly believe anyone would volunteer to do such a thing! But Edie and her husband were on the verge of an empty nest, and her proofreading job only required internet access. Since she often worked at night anyway, plus had the freedom and flexibility to sleep during the day, this worked well for her. We have thanked God over and over for Edie as she has faithfully helped us with one or even two night shifts a week ever since.

CR8050808CR3CR8050808CR

In December 2017, after Verity had lost over a half-pound, bringing her weight down to 12 pounds, 5 ounces, we changed her feeding routine. We had been in and out of our G.I. doctor's office so many times that he had quickly become a vital member of Team Verity. After a litany of tests and careful experiments to see what Verity could tolerate, we agreed a safe next step would be to quit giving bolus feeds every few hours and instead do a slow, continuous feed 24 hours a day. We hoped to prevent a Nissen fundoplication surgery[17] or any other more drastic measures. This turned out to be the answer we

---

[17] In this procedure, the surgeon wraps the top of the stomach around the lower esophagus, making it less likely acid will back up in the esophagus.

needed at that time. The vomiting all but stopped, proving to me that it wasn't my breast milk causing issues but rather the amount she was getting. Her little tummy just could not handle much volume.

Verity gained weight and made some nice developmental strides as we headed toward her first birthday, a milestone we had never been quite sure if we would get to celebrate. A year before, I had nearly driven myself mad with all my worrying and wondering.

What if our baby lives instead of dies?

What if we bring her home from the hospital?

What if we go from parenting 8 healthy kids to adding one more...with special needs?

Well, what did life look like now? Because we were living the IF! I made a list of some things our life included, a life that now felt completely normal. This different kind of normal looked like:

Bottles and pump parts in and around the sink, waiting to be washed or drip drying on the rack.

Once-unfamiliar equipment (feeding pump, pulse oximeter, suction machine) being part of daily life.

An impressive binder and filing system to hold never-ending medical paperwork.

Therapy sessions twice a week and specialty appointments several times a month.

Parents falling asleep in the middle of meetings and movies.

Brothers and sisters coming and going, kissing Verity, playing with her, singing to her.

Jumping up and down when Verity gained a few ounces or reached for a toy.

Cuddle sessions instead of the "shoulds:" I "should" be cleaning; I "should" be working; I "should" be prepping dinner.

As we cleaned and decorated our house in preparation for Verity's huge birthday celebration, I was overcome with emotion and gratitude. Friends and family near and far traveled to be with us, and we had the biggest First Birthday Party we could possibly muster, with the theme "Joy Comes in the Morning." Who would have ever thought we would reach this day? The grim statistics told us 5-10% of Trisomy 18 babies live to their first birthday. A different set of data revealed that of the babies who receive interventions—the same kinds of intervention given to any other children without a T18 diagnosis—35% of those babies will celebrate their first birthday. No matter how we look at it, Verity's life is a miracle, and, just like every other life, it is worth celebrating. And celebrate we did!

Chapter 16

Year Two and Beyond

A night nurse joined Team Verity soon after her first birthday, which was a gift to us, her parents. Miss Jessica immediately became a cherished part of our family, not only because we could get uninterrupted sleep the two or three nights a week she came, but also because she loved Jesus and Verity so completely. I often heard her singing praise songs over our girl. And we appreciated Jessica's prayers as well as her expertise. One night not long after she began working in our home, she had to awaken us to call 911. Verity was turning blue despite all attempts to get her oxygen saturations up. The EMS team arrived in record time, and the breathing treatment they gave Verity helped her get almost back to normal during the ambulance ride to the hospital. It was amazing how a little sniffle turned into something so desperate so fast.[18] She was admitted for general bronchiolitis and spent two nights in the hospital. Because we had oxygen supplies and a pulse oximeter at home, we were discharged sooner than we might otherwise have been.

We had two more hospital stays for illness, both for aspiration pneumonia[19], something we had dreaded but thankfully overcame without too much difficulty. The first such admission came in April 2018, about a month after our terrifying ride in the ambulance, and the second in August. Following the second admission we received a home nebulizer kit, and with that added to all the other tools we have at home, we have not needed to make any other emergency trips for respiratory illness.

Unfortunately, there have been visits to urgent care related to another issue. Verity's anatomy has made her prone to urinary tract infections. She had two in her first year and then went almost 12 months with no problems. But three UTIs in four months led to her being on prophylactic antibiotics. Thankfully she has been UTI-free since.

Verity's feeding routines have also changed considerably since her first birthday when she was still only receiving breast milk. We moved extremely slowly toward bolus (mealtime) feedings while gradually

---

[18] This is a good time to note: if you are sick, please stay home! Fragile immune systems cannot handle germs the way healthier folks can.
[19] When food, stomach acid, or saliva is inhaled into the lungs and results in an infection.

increasing the amount of Nourish (an organic, whole-foods formula) and decreasing the breast milk. After 14 months of pumping, my supply was definitely dwindling, and I have to admit I was ready to quit pumping multiple times a day! Over the course of about three months we transitioned Verity to 100% formula. Even more gradually we worked her up to this, our current feeding routine: three mealtime feedings a day of about three ounces each. These are three hours apart and take approximately a half-hour, although we often pause the feedings halfway because emesis is still an issue. Then Verity receives 40ml per hour in a 15-hour continuous feed. A common question is whether Verity will ever be able to eat orally. We will never rule this out completely; we encourage oral stimulation and offer her tastes of all kinds of things (coconut milk, tomato sauce, pureed soups, applesauce, honey, cheese sauce, and ice cream, for example). However, her tendency to gag and choke has made us extremely cautious even as she has gotten so much better at swallowing overall.

Year One was a year of survival and hoping to keep Verity alive, whereas Year Two brought so many developmental strides. At Verity's first birthday, she was hardly even reaching for toys, showing little to no interest in them. As we transitioned to some bolus feedings, having some tube-free time during daytime hours helped Verity's development tremendously.

Probably the biggest factor in aiding Verity's cognitive awareness came when she was 14 months old. This is when she received her Bone-Assisted Hearing Aid

(BAHA). This is a device on a headband that conducts sound through her skull so she can receive auditory input. Verity had undergone hearing assessments at three months and eleven months of age, the latter under sedation. Both tests confirmed moderate to severe hearing loss, but her hearing organs are normal. As is common with Trisomy 18 children, Verity's ear canals are tiny, with the tissue collapsing in on them. It took us months to get through the assessments and then meet with an audiologist.

Soon after Verity received her BAHA, our early intervention program set us up with a speech therapist. Jen works full-time as a teacher of the deaf in the public schools, but she also adores working with children who have other complications in addition to being deaf or hard of hearing. With her instruction, we began to gain a better understanding of Verity's little world. Jen told us to think of our daughter as a newborn or one-month-old, because that was how long she had been using her BAHA when we began speech therapy. The world of sound was more or less completely new to Verity. We began seeing changes—what we considered to be huge leaps in Verity's development. She began reaching for and interacting with toys. She became more vocal, exploring sounds. And she became noticeably more interactive, responding to the people in her life in more recognizable ways.

I remembered the first few months of her life when I so desperately wanted to see her smile. It seemed our tiny baby was never happy, and it broke my heart. Verity was four months old before she ever broke out in a smile.

Now, with the help of her BAHA and much therapy support, not to mention constant stimulation in our busy household, Verity not only smiles frequently but also laughs and wiggles her body in delight.

Mobility is and always will be a big issue for Verity, so our nurses and therapists continue to work creatively to give her the support she needs to take steps (no pun intended) in this area. As I write this, she is 27 months old and only sits unassisted for seconds at a time. Even so, she has made so much progress! Though still tiny—she just recently passed the 18-pound-mark—her body is much more solid and sturdy. I firmly believe she will walk and maybe even run someday, just as her big sister Kenna envisioned! I've seen some of her Trisomy brothers and sisters walking with the aid of different types of equipment, and it makes me excited for the possibilities. Susan and Christine, our occupational and physical therapists, have been working with Verity in our home for nearly two years now. And our day nurses, Yvette and Janet, have now been with us over a year, working with Verity a total of five days a week and faithfully implementing the many activities and ideas we get during each therapy session. I love the positive attitudes all of these ladies have. I wish the whole world could see our girl through the eyes of her nurses and therapists!

As Verity has grown and changed, the way we attend to her needs has had to change as well. She has had a second tenotomy (tendon release) and will likely need further reconstructive surgery on her feet down the road as we continue to support her in an effort to help her reach her highest potential regarding standing and, Lord willing, walking one day. Additionally, further sleep studies have revealed an increasing number of apnea episodes (a few central, most obstructive) which we must address. We are transitioning from oxygen support via nasal cannula during her sleep to CPAP therapy with a pediatric wisp mask.

We've come so far and learned so much in the past couple of years. The difficult days (and every day used to be incredibly difficult), slogging through whatever the immediate issue happened to be, seem to have morphed into what we would call normal days. Oh, we still have difficult days (and nights). But little did we know in the early days that we would see our Verity smile, roll over, and play with toys; that we would hear her babble and giggle throughout the day; that she would light up seeing Daddy come home from work in the evenings and enjoy silly play time with her siblings. Little did we know our Verity—a child the head neonatologist suggested would lead a "futile life"—would touch so many hearts near and far, including (and especially) our own.

This different kind of normal looks like love
> and laughter
> and living in the moment
> and appreciating the little things.

And yes...sometimes it looks like tears
> and tantrums
> and turmoil
> and terrifying moments.

I can't lie: this isn't an easy life. It's not what we would have chosen. But it IS what we choose now, over and over, day after day. Verity has changed our lives for the better. Being her family means living in the grace and strength of a God who created Verity perfectly, whose plans and purposes reach far beyond our comfort zone. Day by day we find ourselves humbly walking in the path of Christ, who allowed Himself to be broken and poured out on our behalf.

I remember the point during my pregnancy when I realized it was time to stop preparing for Verity to die and start preparing for her to live. And I had to face the fact that her living would look much different than any of our other children's lives. As I scoured the online support groups, I saw many comments from parents of Trisomy children with a common thread: HOPE. Encouragement abounded for anxious mothers like me who couldn't see their way out of the fog of a scary diagnosis. And despite families facing chemo, getting tests done, waiting for answers, preparing for surgeries, caring for little ones through sicknesses at home and in the hospital—in the midst of tests and illnesses and therapies and surgeries—I saw many shining examples of hope.

Hope for Trisomy? Where's the hope in a diagnosis some doctors call "incompatible with life?" Where's the hope for a child who may not reach his or her first birthday? Where's the hope for the parents who are on the brink of despair and exhaustion? For siblings who have to wait for attention because Mom is attending their special-needs sister? Perhaps to a world concerned with image and perfection and beauty, to a world that prioritizes personal freedom over responsibility, a life such as ours would be devoid of hope.

But I'll tell you this: I see hope every day. I see it in the smile of a little girl who didn't smile for months. I see it in the giggles and grins she now gives her brothers and sisters. I see it all over her face when her daddy comes home and sings her special song. I see it in the twinkle in her eyes when she pushes against me, indicating she wants to be rocked. I see it in the kicking of her legs and the workings of her fingers, hands that used to be clenched so tightly she could not open and close them. I see hope in motion as Verity works hard during therapy, doing things we never dreamed she could do a year ago.

I see hope in the form of a wheelchair that will grow with her. I see hope in the form of a committed family chipping in to make sure Verity has what she needs when she needs it. I see hope on the faces of nurses and therapists as they cheer her on each day. I see hope in a medical community at large that is finally starting to understand the potential Trisomy kids have to grow and thrive with proper interventions.

I see hope everywhere Verity's life shines.

And it's a beautiful thing.

Verity Irene is not a scary statistic. She is a beautiful, joyful, playful little girl, and this despite having a much more difficult life than most people will ever have. She completes our family and touches the hearts of strangers. She has made us all better people simply for being part of our lives. When I was pregnant with her, I read similar testimonies from other special-needs families. I clung to those words, other people's stories of love and joy and hope. And slowly I began to dare to believe that maybe, just maybe, someday that would be our story, too.

And now—it is. It has been all along, really. Perhaps we were so busy trying to survive that we didn't realize what was happening: the struggles and fears and difficulties only highlighted the beautiful tapestry woven together with threads of love and joy and hope.

To God be the glory.

Epilogue

It's difficult to know how to end an ongoing story. Only God knows what chapters are still to come, but if I've learned anything over the last couple of decades, it's that I can trust His authorship completely. I will leave off with a snapshot of our Here and Now...

Charis Noelle, our first homeschool graduate, is 18 years old and nearing the completion of a one-year ministry internship at a local church. She plans to attend Colorado Christian University in the fall of 2019 and major in psychology, possibly with a counseling emphasis. Her passions and gifts include public speaking, apologetics, and theology, but she still makes quality time with her little siblings a priority.

Tobin Michael is 17 and completing his junior year of high school. He is most like his father, to include having a quick, punny wit. He is a stellar worker at a local fast food restaurant and leaning toward a career in strategic intelligence and/or criminal justice. Patrick Henry College is high on the list of possible schools, but first he will take cybersecurity classes through the local public schools' partnership with Pikes Peak Community College.

Arden Daniel is 15 and finishing his sophomore year. At the moment he is the tallest member of our family and (almost) completely obsessed with every kind of Rubik's cube he can get his hands on, competing in local competitions for the sheer joy of beating his personal best. He is a leader in a local Good News Club and loves teaching and working with children. His future plans are uncertain but may involve computers or teaching math.

Kenna Joelle, at 12 years old, knows her way around a kitchen and child care far better than I ever did at her age. She can make homemade mayonnaise, egg salad, Italian pasta sauce, and macaroni and cheese like no one's business. She is the only sibling who knows how to attach Verity's extension tube and set up her feedings. Her independent streak as a toddler was frustrating; these days it is a saving grace!

Lucan Thaniel, our resident artist, is 10 years old. His interests and talents include math, piano, Legos, and drawing. He is a highly sensitive boy who feels deeply. Daily he prays for "more and more people to come to know Jesus." His heart for people may very well lead him to the mission field someday; he has talked about sharing the gospel with others since he was 5 or 6 years old.

Zaden Ezekiel, 7 ½, loves Jesus and hates hair-cuts. Like all of our kids, he is a voracious reader and is currently giving me a theatrical reading of *Charlie and the Chocolate Factory* during our time together. I wish I could bottle his initiative: without being asked, the boy cleans, organizes, and generally makes life run more smoothly. His tight squeezes warm my heart.

Seanin Gabriel is 5 ½ with twinkling eyes and a belly laugh that you can't help joining in. He is sweet, silly, and cuddly and loves to eat just about everything except what I've made for dinner (unless it's pizza or pasta: we call him "Captain Carbo"). A current interest is Typing Instructor, but a good-weather day will find him fighting bad guys on the trampoline.

Rhema Riyel turns 4 in a couple of months and is already counting the days until her birthday. She loves giving orders to anyone within earshot, including our nurses. (Sigh.) She is highly verbal and believes herself entirely competent in matters such as Verity's care and matters of personal hygiene. Her interest in all things Verity may lead to a career as a therapist; she is certainly involved in every session!

And Verity Irene. Our little caboose. At 27 months old, she is just as much a cherished part of our family as all of her big brothers and sisters. Every day I look at her and see the word MIRACLE written all over her sweet little self. Our life with her certainly can be challenging, but whatever difficulties we face will not shake our belief that Verity has value and dignity simply because she is created in God's image...extra chromosome and all.

A Word to Anxious Hearts

If you or someone you know is facing an unexpected pregnancy, first of all—congratulations! Life is always worth celebrating. At the same time, I completely understand how frightened and overwhelmed one can feel at the thought of an unplanned pregnancy. Even though I have always had a tremendous support system, and even though my husband is firmly committed to me and to our children, I well remember the feeling of being completely overwhelmed at seeing those two pink lines on yet another pregnancy test.

Take lots of deep breaths and then, when you're ready, tell God all your feelings. He already knows. But pouring out your heart to the One who made you as well as the tiny babe in your womb is the first step to opening the door to receive His blessings. And those blessings may look very, very different from what you wanted to do with your life. Be willing to open up your heart and mind to a greater purpose that will fulfill you beyond your wildest dreams. Next, if you don't already have support, look for a local pregnancy resource center. Trained individuals are ready and waiting to help moms and dads who aren't sure where to turn next.

Likewise, if you or someone you know has received a scary diagnosis for an unborn or recently born child, please know first of all that you are not alone. You're not alone with this specific diagnosis, and you're not alone in feeling all the strange, unfamiliar, and even contradictory emotions that seem to be overtaking your soul. Have courage—dig beyond the statistics and find the families who will become your tribe, those who are already walking the path on which you have been unceremoniously dumped.

Most of all, reach out to the One who created you AND your child. Know that He never makes mistakes. There is purpose far beyond what we can see and touch.

And it is *good*.

Trisomy-Specific Resources

Contrary to outdated medical research and terminology, Trisomy 18 and other rare trisomies are not automatically "incompatible with life." If you or a loved one has received this diagnosis for a baby, please know there is hope and support for families walking this journey.

Support Organization for Trisomy 18, 13, and Related Disorders (SOFT): trisomy.org

Hope for Trisomy: hopefortrisomy13and18.org

International Trisomy Alliance (ITA): internationaltrisomyalliance.com

Facebook Support Group: Rare Trisomy Parents (was T18 Mommies)

A Word from The Word

If you don't yet know Jesus—I mean really KNOW Him—would you take some time to read these messages from His heart to yours? My prayer is for you to know how much God loves you and how you can have a relationship with Him that will last for all eternity.

I have loved you with an everlasting love; I have drawn you with loving-kindness.
Jeremiah 31:3

For God so loved the world that he gave his one and only Son, that whoever believes in him shall not perish but have eternal life. For God did not send his Son into the world to condemn the world, but to save the world through him. Whoever believes in him is not condemned, but whoever does not believe stands condemned already because they have not believed in the name of God's one and only Son.
John 3:16-18

Now we know that whatever the law says, it says to those who are under the law, so that every mouth may be silenced and the whole world held accountable to God. Therefore no one will be declared righteous in his sight by observing the law; rather, through the law we become conscious of sin. But now a righteousness from God, apart from law, has been made known, to which the Law and the Prophets testify. This righteousness from God comes through faith in Jesus Christ to all who believe. There is no difference, for all have sinned and fall short of the glory of God, and are justified freely by his grace through the redemption that came by Christ Jesus.
Romans 3:19-24

As it is written: "There is no one righteous, not even one."
Romans 3:10

God made him who had no sin to be sin for us, so that in him we might become the righteousness of God.
2 Corinthians 5:21

You see, at just the right time, when we were still powerless, Christ died for the ungodly. Very rarely will anyone die for a righteous man, though for a good man someone might possibly dare to die. But God demonstrates his own love for us in this: While we were still sinners, Christ died for us.
Romans 5:6-8

For it is by grace you have been saved through faith—and this not from yourselves, it is the gift of God—not by works, so that no one can boast. For we are God's workmanship, created in Christ Jesus to do good works, which God prepared in advance for us to do.
Ephesians 2:8-10

That if you confess with your mouth, "Jesus is Lord," and believe in your heart that God raised him from the dead, you will be saved. For it is with your heart that you believe and are justified, and it is with your mouth that you confess and are saved.
Romans 10:9-10

He...asked, "Sirs, what must I do to be saved?"
They replied, "Believe in the Lord Jesus, and you will be saved—you and your household."
Acts 16:31

But these are written that you may believe that Jesus is the Christ, the Son of God, and that by believing you may have life in his name.
John 20:31

For I am convinced that neither death nor life, neither angels nor demons, neither the present nor the future, nor any powers, neither height nor depth, nor anything else in all creation, will be able to separate us from the love of God that is in Christ Jesus our Lord.
Romans 8:38-39

Proceeds from the sales of this book will be used for a special project: Verity's Village, currently existing as a dream in the author's mind, will one day be a ministry and resource center for special-needs families. Thank you for helping bring this dream to life!

Made in the USA
Columbia, SC
20 August 2019